D1442479

BEADING WITH FILIGREE

BEADING WITH FILIGREE

Beautiful Jewelry, Simple Techniques

Cynthia Deis

LARK BOOKS

A Division of Sterling Publishing Co., Inc.
New York / London

Senior Editor
Valerie Van Arsdale Shrader

Art Director
Stacey Budge

Cover Designer
Cindy LaBreacht

Production Editor
Nathalie Mornu

Copy Editor
Jean Campbell

Illustrator
J'aime Allene

Photographer
Stewart O'Shields

Author Photo
Kurt Schlatzer

Library of Congress Cataloging-in-Publication Data

Deis, Cynthia.
  Beading with filigree : beautiful jewelry, simple techniques / Cynthia
Deis. -- 1st ed.
    p. cm.
  Includes index.
  ISBN-13: 978-1-60059-187-7 (hc-plc with jacket : alk. paper)
  ISBN-10: 1-60059-187-6 (hc-plc with jacket : alk. paper)
  1. Jewelry making. 2. Beadwork. 3. Wire craft. 4. Filigree. I. Title.
  TT212.D445 2008
  739.27--dc22

                                                        2007048728

10 9 8 7 6 5 4 3 2 1

First Edition

Published by Lark Books, A Division of
Sterling Publishing Co., Inc.
387 Park Avenue South, New York, NY 10016

Text © 2008, Cynthia Deis
Photography © 2008, Lark Books
Illustrations © 2008, Lark Books

Distributed in Canada by Sterling Publishing,
c/o Canadian Manda Group, 165 Dufferin Street
Toronto, Ontario, Canada M6K 3H6

Distributed in the United Kingdom by GMC Distribution Services,
Castle Place, 166 High Street, Lewes, East Sussex, England BN7 1XU

Distributed in Australia by Capricorn Link (Australia) Pty Ltd.,
P.O. Box 704, Windsor, NSW 2756 Australia

If you have questions or comments about this book, please contact:
Lark Books
67 Broadway
Asheville, NC 28801
828-253-0467

Manufactured in China

ISBN 13: 978-1-60059-187-7

For information about custom editions, special sales, and premium and corporate
purchases, please contact Sterling Special Sales Department at 800-805-5489
or specialsales@sterlingpub.com.

Contents

I remember a beaded filigree hair comb that sat in a jewelry box in my Aunt Judy's house. She was glamorous and generous, her baubles weren't too precious to touch, and the silver comb had a bit of beading along the rim. It's my first memory of filigree. I was enthralled with the curled metal lace, wishing my sparse hair could hold that comb. As I got older, I saw in books and old-fashioned magazines that filigree had been popular for a very long time. The shapes and forms from various eras were somewhat similar, but different combinations of beads or finish resulted in a completely changed look.

I noticed filigree again and again in antique shops and dusty flea markets. I collected broken bits, combining them to make jewelry that mixed vintage and new elements, but didn't think of turning my obsession with sparkle into a business until 1996. At the time, I created displays at a clothing boutique, and eventually worked up the courage to approach the buyer about carrying my jewelry. She agreed to look at my "line." I didn't have one, really—just a dozen or so necklaces in an old velveteen box. I hoped to trade them for the shoes I had placed on lay-away. I showed up for our appointment with nothing but my designs. The buyer patiently gave me paper and pen to take her order, and I walked home elated, with my first commission!

I started showing my samples at other boutiques, and continued to poke around antique stores, occasionally coming across a container of unused filigree dangles or rosettes. One weathered, illegible box bore the name of a filigree manufacturer. Imagine my joy when I discovered it was still in business! The company directed me to many places that supplied filigree, and when the catalogs arrived, I was delirious at the variety of shapes I'd never seen before, and many I recognized, too. My jewelry collection became a real line, which I began selling to department stores and catalog companies as far away as Japan and France.

This book reflects pieces I created for my jewelry line, Bedizen Ornaments, and designs that re-create antique pieces from my collection. While some projects may seem trendy or new to you, they're really old favorites. Golden Shimmer (page 118) is very similar to pieces that adorned the necks of Art Nouveau beauties almost a hundred years ago, and Helen (shown at left and on page 121) could have been worn by a chic Park Avenue socialite in the 1950s. Over time, filigree has remained consistently fashionable and consistently feminine. Changes in beads or metal finish allow the versatile shapes and timeless motifs to be "on trend" every season.

In case you're curious about this beautiful material, I describe it in the Filigree Primer. I then tell you about all the other materials and tools you'll need in a section called Getting Started; if you've made jewelry before, you're likely to have many of these items on hand. My construction methods are explained in the Basic Techniques section. It's best to familiarize yourself with these processes before making any of the 33 projects that follow.

Although I've designed most of the projects in this book specifically for the beads and filigree pieces listed in the instructions, you may want to make substitutions, and should feel free to do so. The Susan brooch (page 62) or Pearl Pointe ring (page 42), for example, would look entirely different with changes in beads or filigree shapes, and the Paisley necklace (page 86) would be the perfect home for a family photo or stone cabochon.

Don't hesitate to experiment with the projects in this book to make them your own. Play around with the different ways of bending and beading filigree. You'll see that you, too, can create trendy yet enduring designs from a classic material that has always proven to be of the moment.

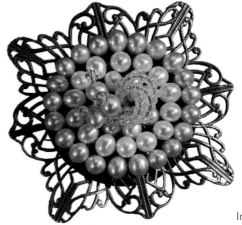

Filigree Primer

Think of your favorite lace, maybe the cuff of a blouse or the trim on a wedding dress. Now imagine those delicate twists and intricate swirls translated into wire. The appeal of filigree lies in that contrast—the juxtaposition of dainty lace shapes wrought in tough, durable metal.

What Is Filigree?

Filigree is as old as metalworking itself. In the hot deserts of ancient Egypt and Mesopotamia, for example, artisans worked with simple tools and fires stoked to tremendous heat by slaves to create filigree pieces of amazing intricacy. Drawing a thin, even wire down from a strip of hand-wrought metal took days, as the craftsmen carefully pulled and heated the metal repeatedly. Each pull stretched the length and thinned the metal, and hammering rounded the wire until the artisan was rewarded with a fine metallic filament. The wire could then be braided, twisted, or looped to form a sort of lace, one far more durable than any made of linen or cotton fiber. (In later forms of filigree, the wires were fused with silver dust, making them even stronger.) This work decorated the heads and necks of just the ruling classes, since only the wealthy could afford to wear an item that took weeks of skilled labor to produce.

Filigree exists in some form in all human civilizations that have worked metal. Most often made of silver (although some cultures used gold), the artifacts of Asia, the Middle East, South America, Africa, and Europe include diverse items decorated with filigree: figurines, belts, reliquaries, tiny purses, spoon handles—and of course, all sorts of adornments, from clasps and buttons to headpieces and jewelry. The tradition persists to this day around the world. Hand-wrought pieces continue to be intensely laborious, requiring days to make even with machine-made wire, gas torches, and electric tools for coiling and looping.

The back of a vintage button

Clockwise from left: a Turkish pendant bought in the mid-1960s; a contemporary Chinese bracelet with Mongolian and Russian influences; a chainmail purse with a filigree lid, found in an English antique store

Stamped Filigree

So how did we get from the handmade to machine-stamped filigree? We can thank the wives of Parisian doctors and London stockbrokers. In the bustling days of the early industrial revolution, the emerging merchant and middle classes clamored for the finer things once reserved for nobility. The introduction of mechanized means of production made this possible. Fine adornments, once reserved for the residents of the palace and the chateau, were copied and produced by stamping out lacy bits of filigree from solid sheets of metal.

The process was relatively simple. A block of iron, called a die, was carved with a pattern of curves and arabesques; placed in a press, the die punched out the negative shapes of the filigree from a thin sheet of metal. Today's powerful, mechanized presses make a loud thunk and whoosh as they stamp out the metal, but in the French workshop of the late 1700s, the machine would have been hand cranked by a young apprentice or two, grunting and exerting themselves mightily.

Since its invention, stamped filigree has been used widely in costume and production jewelry. Look carefully at Victorian portraits and you'll spot stamped filigree beaded with complex patterns of jet beads. Under their bobbed hair, flappers sported dangly earrings with sparkling filigree bead caps. Pearl-accented filigree adorned the necks of the torch singers of the 1930s and 1940s, and the beaded button-style earrings favored by housewives in post-war suburbia were based on filigree rosettes. Because it's pretty in and of

itself but readily accepts beads or accents, filigree was and is still a popular feature in jewelry.

Metal filigree continues to be produced using steel dies, in many cases the same ones that first stamped out their metal lace more than a century ago. The production is highly mechanized so that a single machine can produce thousands of pieces in a day. Factories in the United States and France manufacture most of the stampings sold worldwide.

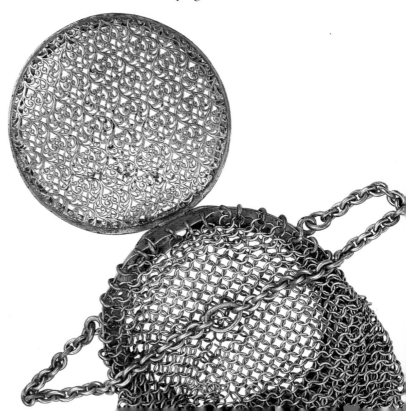

Types of Metal

Stamped filigree pieces are available in a variety of metals, but they're most often made from brass, a highly malleable alloy of copper and zinc with trace amounts of nickel. In its natural state, brass has an appealing golden finish, but when left unsealed, the air gives it a rich bronze patina. Brass can also be plated easily to resemble sterling silver, gold, or copper.

Raw or *natural brass* filigree is unplated and will range in color from bright gold to a deep bronze. If you like the color of raw brass, seal it to maintain the color. If you wish to darken or antique the brass you can apply heat with a torch, gas stove, or kiln to darken the metal (see page 30).

In *antiqued brass* filigree, the metal is darkened with heat or chemicals, and then the finish is sealed with a skin-safe lacquer. It has a warm patina and is often my first choice when using brass findings. Antiquing does not cause the metal to stiffen and the lacquer can easily be burned off if you desire a raw metal surface.

Plated brass filigree is available in a variety of finishes. Because plating of any metal increases the hardness of the core metal and adds an additional, stiff layer—the plating—these components will be slightly more brittle than their unplated brass counterparts. Care must be taken if bending or forming plated filigree so that the finish doesn't crack or flake off. Keep in mind that bending this type of filigree too much can result in breakage.

Like other brass filigree, plated finishes can be heat-treated and painted (page 31).

Solid sterling silver or *gold* stamped filigree is very rarely available, but it can be used in many of the same ways as brass filigree. Pure metals like sterling silver or gold are more flexible than alloys such as brass, so these elements will bend quite easily. Do note that twisted wire filigree should not be bent, because pressure applied to soldered joints and wire twists can cause breakage.

Filigree Shapes

Filigree components come in an assortment of shapes, ranging from tiny teardrops to large flowers to beads. From item to item, you'll frequently see the same shapes replicated and repeated. For instance, a small, filigreed teardrop might also appear as the petal of a large flower, or three of the teardrops might be grouped together as a fan. Filigree forms are often symmetrical, drawing from decorative motifs seen in textiles and architecture as well as stylized natural forms. The symmetry of filigree is also an expression of manufacturing limits and functional uses. Creating a design takes time and it's more efficient to tweak an existing shape and die than to come up with an entirely new one. Producing a shape in a variety of sizes also makes it versatile; a design of filigree pieces stacked and attached to make earrings translates well into a set by using larger identical elements, also stacked and attached, for a necklace pendant.

Not only does a wide array of flat shapes exist, but filigree is also available in three-dimensional shapes. Some are bowed, some are cupped, and others still are completely spherical to form beads. The shaping, when accomplished by a machine, is called *dapping*, and it generally takes place before any plating or surface finish is applied. Machine dapping creates elements that are slightly stiffer than flat filigree, but the trade-off is smooth, complex curves or sharp folds. Bead caps, for example, begin life as flat rosettes, and curved fans start out as flat triangles of filigree.

Dapped pieces can be mixed and combined with flat pieces to produce layered effects. I did this with Lotus (page 101) and Elizabeth (page 78), for example. You can also hand-bend flat components to give them simple curves, as I did on the links for Pavlova (page 36). I explain how to make these types of bends on page 28.

Getting Started

Metal filigree can be vintage or graphic, elaborate or simple. It's strong and malleable and you'll find that you can transform the look of just about any type of filigree shape using beads, ribbon, or paint to create a look that's all your own. I love using filigree in my designs because it lends a historical touch, but can it still look completely contemporary. You may have never thought of using filigree in your own jewelry, but I hope you fall in love with filigree the way I did while creating the projects in this book.

Creating beaded jewelry using filigree components as the base is relatively easy to do, but it does require some basic know-how. First, you'll want to learn about all the materials on your shopping list. Then, read up on tools to find out what gadgets you'll need at your design station. Get some good ideas on setting up your work-space. And finally, go on to the next section to find all the basic techniques you need to know to make each project. You'll be on your way to making stunning filigree jewelry in no time.

Materials

Filigree is beautiful in its own right, but adding the glitz and glamour of beads brings it up another notch. Here's more information about beads and the other materials you need to create sensational beaded filigree jewelry.

Bead Sizing

In *Beading with Filigree*, most beads are described in metric measurements, the initial measurement from hole to hole. For instance, a 6 x 8-mm bead is 6 mm from hole to hole and 8 mm wide. Round beads are measured with one number: 3 mm, 4 mm, etc. For seed bead sizing, see the box on page 14.

Beads and Stones

Beads come in a dizzying variety of sizes and shapes. Because matching specific beads can be difficult, I've specified sizes for all the beads used in the projects in this book. But please do yourself a favor—be creative as you make your own projects, and don't be afraid to try out different color combinations than the ones I suggest.

Cabochons and *glass bevels* are used in this book for setting into bent filigree. They have domed tops and flat backs, and are available in a variety of stone types and glass colors. Look for smooth, unscratched tops when purchasing. Glass buttons with the shank removed can be used in place of cabochons. Jewelry insiders and bead geeks will sometimes call cabochons 'cabs' when they are showing off.

Crystal beads are very sparkly and are ideal when you want to add maximum glitter to your projects. You can substitute similarly sized machine-cut crystal or Czech fire-polished glass for any project. *Rhinestone flat backs* are clear or colored crystals with mirrored backs set into metal. They add an extra bit of sparkle to any jewelry project and can be attached to filigree by sewing (see page 26).

Crystal beads

Crystal pearl beads are man-made pearls available in 2- to 40-mm sizes. I often work with crystal pearls because of their even finish and realistic weight.

Czech fire-polished glass beads are round, slightly oval, or rondelle-shaped beads with facets on the sides. They have a lovely sparkle and are widely available at bead stores and bead shows. My favorite sizes for beading with filigree are 3, 4, 6, and 8 mm. I buy five or six strands of a color I like whenever I see them. These beads vary in color and finish and may be opaque, translucent, or transparent. Sometimes you'll find a type of Czech fire-polished bead that mixes a variety of colors and finishes called *givré* (pronounced gee-vray.) I use givré fire-polished beads in several projects in this book.

Fire-polished beads

Givré beads

Cabochons come in various shapes and sizes.

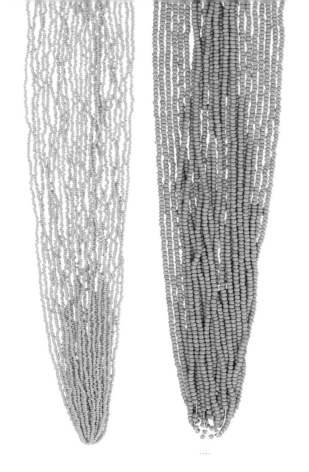

Czech pressed glass beads are available in a variety of shapes and sizes, including iconic shapes such as leaves, faces, hearts, etc. Many vintage glass beads are Czech pressed glass. *Druks* are round pressed glass beads.

Natural pearl beads are a lovely choice for working with filigree. Look for consistent openings and smooth luster. I will always buy a strand of tiny freshwater pearls in a favorite color to have on hand for including in a beaded project. If you are making your work to sell, freshwater pearls are popular with jewelry buyers.

Seed Bead Sizing

Seed beads have their own nomenclature when size is in question. The bead size goes up as the bead size number goes down. This means a size 6° ("six-aught" or "six-0") seed bead is larger than a size 12° bead. If you're wondering why seed bead numbers get larger as the beads themselves get smaller, it's helpful to think of the way seed beads are made. A thin, hollow tube of glass, about the diameter of a pencil, is stretched repeatedly and then cut into small sections that are then tumbled to make the rounded seed beads. Each stretch makes the glass tube thinner and longer. This is why the beads get smaller as the numbers get larger. A 6° seed bead was stretched six times, while an 8° bead got stretched eight times.

Seed beads are made by cutting tiny tubes of glass and then tumble-polishing until the beads are smooth. They are sized from under a millimeter to 5 mm long. For the projects that include seed beads in this book, I've primarily used sizes 8° to 11°. ***Note:*** Seed beads that have been cut with one facet are called *charlottes*. I prefer the more sparkly size 9° three-cut seed beads for filigree projects, although any seed bead can be substituted. Japanese cylinder beads can also be used, but I prefer the rounded edges of the tumbled Czech beads for embellishing filigree.

Semiprecious stone beads are made from natural stone in a range of sizes, shapes, and finishes. Any of the designs in this book can be made with stone beads in the appropriate sizes. Look for large holes that will take the beading wire you wish to use.

Left to right: bead caps, lobster clasps, spring ring clasps, hooks

Findings

Any metal parts you use in making jewelry are commonly called *findings*. Clasps, jump rings, ear wires, and other metal parts are available in the same variety of finishes as filigree, and you can choose to match your filigree or mix your metals. Don't be afraid to combine colors if you can't find an exact match! Mixed metal jewelry is very sophisticated and by including several colors of metal you can add visual interest to your work. A simple way to make your mixed metal designs flow is to remember to repeat and alternate the metals; if you use a silver clasp with copper filigree you should also use silver jump rings between the filigree pieces. Of you could use brass chain and charms, mixing copper and silver jump rings with a toggle that is half copper, half silver. I've mixed metals in the Coral Blossom pin (page 53) in this way.

Bead caps are often flower- or leaf-shaped metal domes, or 'caps,' that accent and enhance beads. The size of bead caps is generally given as an outside measurement *or* the size of the bead the cap is designed to fit.

Knot covers are small clamshell-shaped metal findings that are used to cover knots or crimps in designs. I use them to finish strands of beads strung on silk or cord.

Clasps are available in many styles, and I've used box, hook, lobster claw, spring ring, and toggle styles for the projects in this book. When selecting a clasp, make sure it has a secure hold and won't slip open.

Crimp covers are small open beads that slip around crimped beads and close with chain-nose pliers. They are used to hide crimped beads, allowing the attachment to blend into a design.

Mixing It Up

Toggles are simple clasps that consist of a ring and a bar. You can use a commercial set like the one shown at right, but for a unique look, I like to make my own by mixing toggle parts from a variety of sets. I sometimes use standard toggle bars with filigree rings, or filigree bars with rings made of beads and wire. See the Carla necklace (below and page 98) for an example of a mixed-up toggle.

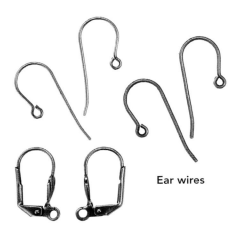

Ear wires

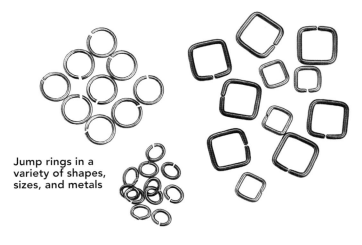

Jump rings in a variety of shapes, sizes, and metals

Crimp beads are tiny, seamless metal beads that are used for finishing strung beads. Look for crimp beads that match the metal in your project and make sure they are seamless. Don't economize on crimps, or your designs may end up in pieces on the floor.

Ear posts and *ear wires* are findings for pierced ears. They come in a variety of metal finishes and range from simple French hooks to the more complex lever-back (sometimes called Euro-wires). For those with allergies, I suggest using sterling or gold-filled ear wires and creating mixed metal pieces by using, say, antiqued copper filigree with sterling jump rings and sterling ear wires.

Head pins are lengths of wire with a tiny ball or "head" that keeps the bead from slipping off. They are sold by length and gauge (width). Head pins with decorative ends are also available; look for pearls, crystals, metal flowers, or leaves. ***Note:*** Plated head pins are more brittle than their unplated counterparts.

Jump rings are sold in millimeter sizes that represent the interior measurement. Various gauges (widths) of wire are used to make jump rings, from thick (18- to 20-gauge) to thin (22- to 24-gauge.) I'm fond of oval jump rings for attaching filigree pieces as they are more subtle than round jump rings. Using a decorative jump ring of any kind will always add a bit of extra interest to your designs, but I really like square jump rings for their unusual shape. If you can't locate them, you should substitute round jump rings or decorative chain links of similar sizes for the designs in this book.

Pin or *brooch backs* are often available with a beading screen or without. These flat metal forms have a soldered pin attached to them and cover the back of a project, turning it into a pin or brooch. The screens can be saved for another project if you have to purchase the sets.

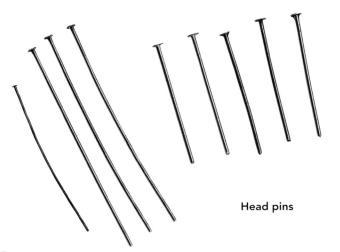

Head pins

Chain

For many of the designs in this book I've relied on chain, not only for hanging pendants or attaching dangles, but also as a source of extra-thick jump rings. Any chain with 'open' or unsoldered links can be separated into many individual rings to be used in your projects. See the Barcelona necklace (page 39) for an example of this.

If you like the matched look, keep your eye open for filigree chain. *Natural* or *raw brass chain* can be used as is or you can alter the finish as discussed on page 30. When buying plated metal chain, look for an even finish. Avoid purchasing chain from a hardware store, as the finish may not be safe for wearing—it's made for lamps and gates, not bracelets and earrings!

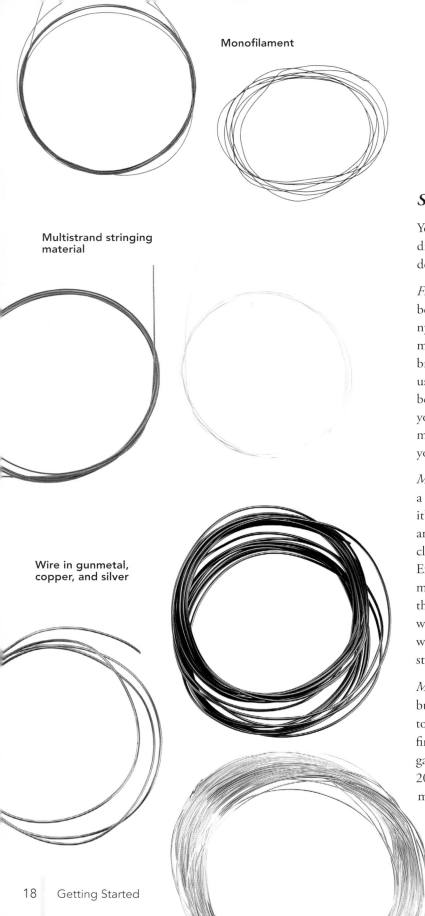

Monofilament

Multistrand stringing material

Wire in gunmetal, copper, and silver

Stringing Materials

You'll find that in *Beading with Filigree* I've used several different types of stringing materials to connect, sew, and decorate filigree.

Flexible beading wire is used in this book for both stringing beads and for sewing beads to filigree (see page 26). It's a nylon-coated multi-strand steel cable wire that has a remarkable drape. Flexible beading wire is sold under several brand names and comes in many different colors. When used for stringing, this wire can be finished with crimp beads (see page 28). When used for sewing beads to filigree you can secure it with a tight square knot (page 27). Always match the color of your stringing material to the filigree you're using.

Memory wire is a stiff steel jewelry-making wire that holds a tight curve. Available in necklace, bracelet, and ring sizes, it's useful for creating short 'choker' style necklaces that are actually comfortable to wear. The wire holds the beads close to the base of the neck without fastening it too tight. Experiment with stringing almost any style of beads on memory wire, but be aware that it's thicker in diameter than many stringing materials, so won't accommodate items with very small holes, such as freshwater pearls. Memory wire must be cut with a special cutting tool, as it's made of steel and will dent or bend even heavy-duty wire cutters.

Metal wire is mostly used in this book to make bead links, but you can also use very thin metal wire to sew beads to filigree. Metal wire is available in many types, colors, finishes, and gauges. Keep in mind that the larger the gauge number, the thinner the wire. In this book I've used 20- and 24-gauge wire for most projects. I generally like to match the wire to the filigree and findings I'm using. Or I select a specific color of wire that will accent the mix of metals I use. It works best to store your wire coils loose, labeled with gauge and separated by metal type.

Ribbon is used in this book to lend a textural element to filigree and as a closure. Experiment with different colors and types to come up with your own style. Trim ribbons and cut knotting thread with scissors. Find a nice sharp pair and keep them away from small children or anyone else who wants to cut construction paper with them!

Other Supplies

There are quite a few other supplies used in *Beading with Filigree* that don't quite fit under a neat heading, but are just as important as the rest.

Epoxy glue is an ideal way to secure pin or earring findings or to seal knots. I always date the glue tube or bottle when I open it and discard it after 12 months. Old glues are prone to cracking, undermining the structural integrity of a piece. Choose a brand of glue that dries clear. Avoid cyanoacrylate glues that can fog the finish on beads and pearls. Always use glues in a well-ventilated area.

Paint can change the look of filigree dramatically. Any enamel spray paint will do. A rainbow of colors is available at both paint and hardware stores. Always spray in a well-ventilated area.

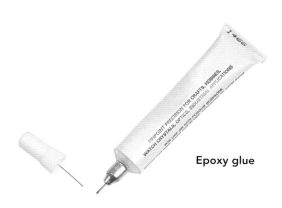

Epoxy glue

Spray paints

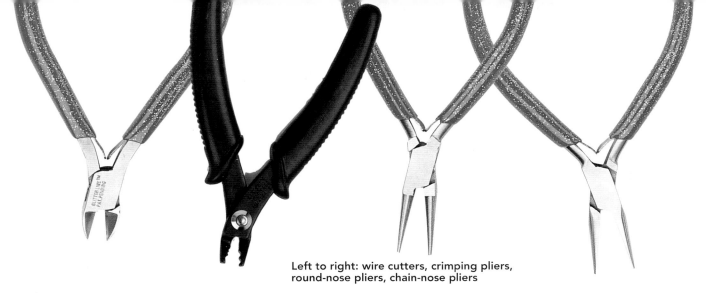

Left to right: wire cutters, crimping pliers, round-nose pliers, chain-nose pliers

Tools

To create the projects in this book you will need a basic set of beading and jewelry-making tools, plus a few unusual items. When purchasing your tools, buy them at your local bead or jewelry-supply store if possible. You'll be able to hold the tools to see if they're comfortable in your hand, and the staff at most stores can give you information on how to use them correctly. Learning to use the tools properly will help you avoid fatigue and strain and make sure you can continue beading for years to come.

Chain-nose pliers are small pliers with narrow, flat tips. You'll use these to bend filigree or wire and to open and close jump rings. While it might seem easy to get these in the garage or at the hardware store, don't be fooled. The hardware store version of this tool, called needle-nose pliers, has teeth that will mar the surface of any filigree or wire you work with. Chain-nose pliers are made for jewelry and craft uses, so they have smooth jaws. You'll need two pairs of these to open and close jump rings.

Round-nose pliers are small pliers with two round tips. You'll use these to create wire loops and to bend filigree into smooth curves. You need to keep at least one pair of these on hand, but they do come in different sizes so you may want to splurge and buy several pairs for your work table. Round-nose pliers with cutters built into them are called *rosary pliers* and are a good option, but you'll probably want another pair of regular wire cutters, too.

Crimping pliers have two special openings designed to close seamless crimp beads securely. See the crimping instructions on page 28 for instructions on how to use these pliers, or visit your local bead store for a hands-on lesson.

Wire cutters or *nippers* are for cutting wire, stringing materials, and filigree. I use two different styles of wire cutters on a daily basis; a very sharp, fine-point pair for cutting stringing materials and fine wire (24-gauge or thinner), and a pair of larger cutters that are better for cutting filigree pieces and thicker-gauge wire. You can ruin fine-tip nippers by cutting material that is too hard or too thick, so be sure to ask when you purchase your cutters what they're made for. There are also *memory wire cutters* made especially for cutting that eternally-coiled steel wire. Since memory wire is made with such hard metal, it can damage regular cutters. This tool snaps the wire instead of cutting it.

Dowels or *rolling pins* are helpful for forming filigree into smoothly curved shapes. You can also look in your kitchen drawers for wooden spoons and spatulas. You might even find that a table or chair leg does the trick, too. I've even formed filigree with a child-sized rolling pin sneaked out of my daughter's toys!

Miniature rolling pin

Workspace

Getting your beading area set up to be functional and creative is important. My workspace is in a sunny room in my house. I have a table with rolling chairs, storage for my supplies, and several cork boards where I can pin up bead samples, photos, and works in progress. Before you get too jealous, I should tell you that I share this workspace with my two young children, so it also contains puzzles and glitter paint. But I find I'm a bit of stickler for wanting things to look "just so," so it really ends up being my space and, with a little help from all my organizational gizmos, I find it easy to be inspired by the shapes and colors that surround me.

Storage

To make my supplies easy to see while I'm working and easy to move out of the way when my children get the spirit to create, I use a combination of storage containers. Clear plastic boxes with hinged lids hold beads and findings sorted by color for long-term storage, but I don't like the look of them when I am creating. I transfer my material selections for specific projects to vintage saucers and tea plates that I purchase at flea markets. The round saucers are just right for the assortment of beads that will become my next design and I like the look of a collection of tiny plates on my work table, like a colorful snack. The clear storage boxes stack on high shelves, above tiny hands, and the saucers can also be placed out of the way if needed.

I store my tools right where I can see them in a vintage test-tube holder, but you can create your own easy tool holder by perching your tools on the edge of a terra cotta pot and using the center to hold spools of wire and stringing materials. Other tool caddies can be found in bead stores, at bead shows, and even in your local cookware store. Find one that works for you and has extra spaces because you'll add more tools as your skills progress.

Work Surface

If you can, start with a sturdy table that's the right height to sit at comfortably, avoiding back strain. I place several non-rolling beading mats on the table and add shallow beading trays to the mix. As designs progress from the saucer stage—just parts—to the bead tray stage—parts laid out in a design—I may take several days to decide on the exact placement. I like to work on several designs at one time so that I can shift gears if I get stuck on a particular design.

Lighting

Good lighting is very important for a work area. My studio is located in the brightest room in the house, but I still need additional lighting for cloudy days or late-night beading. Full spectrum lights are widely available and some even come with clip-on magnifiers to make your work easier to see. I also have a vintage 1960s drafting table lamp that I had retrofitted with a full spectrum light bulb. It fits my criteria of looking just right for the space and is functional as well.

Don't Worry!

No matter what space is available to you, take a bit of time to make sure it's both functional and inspirational. Don't worry if you don't have the perfect space to get started. Find an area with a comfortable chair and good lighting and the rest—all the saucers and tool holders—will happen. In the meantime you can create beautiful jewelry to wear while you're setting up your ideal studio!

Basic Techniques

Beaded filigree jewelry may seem complicated to make, but even the most elaborate projects in this book can be broken down into simple steps using basic techniques. Read through this chapter so you understand these techniques and you'll soon be making and wearing your very own gorgeous jewelry.

Wire Looping

Wire looping techniques are incorporated in just about every project in this book and are primarily used to make bead dangles, bead links, and beaded chain. First learn how to make the two varieties of wire loops, simple and wrapped, then go on to learn how to incorporate the technique. You'll be an expert in no time.

Simple Loop

This loop is not completely secure, but is versatile because it can be opened after it's been formed. Once you've made one, refer to the directions for "Opening and Closing Rings" (page 25) to learn how to open a simple loop properly.

1. Slide your bead onto the head pin or wire. Make sure you have at least ⅜ inch (9 mm) of wire to make the loop. If you are working on top of a bead, use wire cutters to trim the wire or head pin to ⅜ inch (9 mm). Use your fingers to bend the wire to a 90° angle (photo 1).

2. Use round-nose pliers to grasp the tip of the wire or head pin. Roll the wire toward you, making a full circle (photo 2).

photo 1

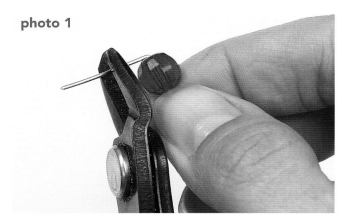

photo 2

Bead Link

Bead links are used to make connectors and are the components in beaded chain (see below).

1. Cut the required amount of wire. Form a simple loop at one end, then slip on one or more beads. Snug the bead(s) to the first loop and trim the wire to ⅜ inch (9 mm) from the last bead strung. Use chain-nose pliers or your fingers to make a 90° bend at the top of the bead (photo 3).

2. Use round-nose pliers to form a second simple loop (photo 4). The completed loops should sit close to the top of the beads. If necessary, grip each completed loop with a pair of chain-nose pliers and twist to make the loops face the same direction.

photo 3   **photo 4**

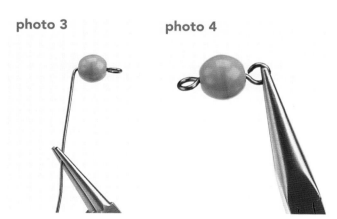

Beaded Chain

Attaching bead links together makes a very attractive custom chain.

1. Make the amount of bead links required, following the steps above.

2. Open one simple loop on a link. Attach the open link to a closed loop on another link. Close the loop. Repeat to finish the required chain length.

Wrapped Loop

This is a very secure loop that can't be opened once created. If you need to attach a wrapped loop to a finding, slip the finding on the loop in step 2 before you make the coil.

1. Grip a piece of wire with round-nose pliers, ¾ inch (1.9 cm) from the end. Form a loop by bending the wire around the tip of the pliers (photo 5).

2. Remove the round-nose pliers and hold the loop itself in chain-nose pliers. Twist the wire ends around each other one and a half times, keeping the longer wire facing straight down from the loop. Trim away the shorter wire, close to the twist (photo 6). Slide on the bead or finding you wish to use.

3. Make the second part of the wrapped loop by bending the wire at a 45° angle and repeating the process of looping on this side of the bead (photo 7). Wrap the wire end around to secure it, then trim off any extra wire close to the twist (photo 8).

photo 5

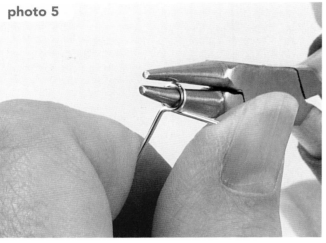

photo 6

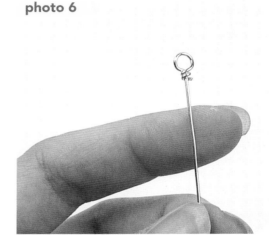

photo 7

photo 8

Opening and Closing Rings

Jump rings are ideal for attaching filigree pieces to each other or to chain, and are natural for adding dangles or charms to a piece. They don't draw attention to themselves. They are secure, but flexible. I love to use oval jump rings when they are available for the extra strength and smooth look they provide, but round jump rings work just as well.

It's very important to open and close jump rings correctly or you'll end up with weakened wire that can snap in two, especially with brass. *Note:* The same instructions below apply to opening and closing simple chain links, finding loops (as with ear wires), and simple loops.

1. Grasp the ring with two pairs of chain-nose pliers, the split in the top of the ring between the pliers.

2. Push one pair of pliers away from you and the other toward you to twist the ring open, as shown in photo 9.

3. To close the ring, just reverse the movement made in step 2. *Note:* Never bend the sides of the ring outward from the split; this just deforms the ring and you will never get it back to the nice round shape it had before. If you end up deforming a jump ring, it's often better to use a new ring instead of trying to salvage the deformed one.

photo 9

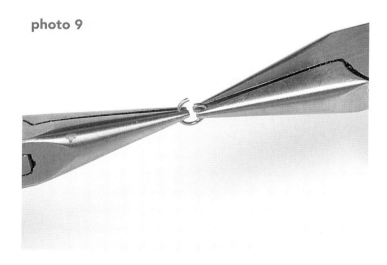

photo 10

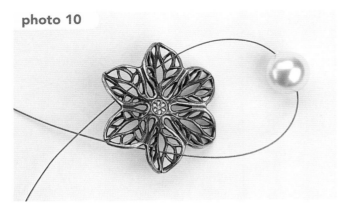

photo 11

photo 12

photo 13

Sewing Beads to Filigree

I like to attach beads to filigree by sewing them on with flexible beading wire. The wire knots so nicely and doesn't hurt my fingers. Always try to match the color of the wire to the filigree. This will ensure that any exposed sewing blends in and isn't noticed, much like matching your thread when sewing on a button! This technique can create a mess on the back of the filigree with the knots and tail strands everywhere, so I always try to cover my knotting with another piece of filigree as in the Blossoms hair pins project, page 76.

1. Cut the required amount of beading wire.

2. String on one bead, leaving a 4-inch (10.2-cm) tail. Working from the front of the filigree, push both ends of the wire through the filigree holes where specified in the instructions (photo 10).

3. Tie a secure square knot (see page 27) on the back of the filigree (photo 11).

4. Pass the long end of the wire up through the filigree to exit where specified (photo 12). Slip on a bead and pass the wire down through the filigree to the back of the filigree.

5. Repeat this sewing action until the filigree is beaded as required (photo 13). Tie the wire ends together in a tight square knot and trim. If you are worried about your knots holding, you can add a drop of glue, but I rarely do this.

Designing Your Own Bead-sewing Patterns

Most filigree pieces are created with even patterns that make them ideal for beading. For instance, the repeated shapes in a filigreed flower or star suggest their own beading patterns because the design naturally repeats. So, when I make my own filigree jewelry designs, the filigree patterns make bead placement easy because I just look for those repetitive filigree lines. They show where I can bead an individual section, and then repeat the beaded pattern across the filigree. And, because the stiff metal supports even rather heavy or ornate beading, I know I can bead to my heart's delight.

While I have used some very common filigree pieces in the projects in this book, you may want or need to make substitutes from time to time. The beading counts in this book are for the styles of filigree specified, but you can easily alter them for the filigree you have available. Don't be afraid to experiment with the styles you have available and mix up the techniques to create your own.

Knotting

You'll need to know how to knot stringing material and ribbon when working on the projects in this book.

An *overhand knot* (figure 1) is made by forming a loop in a single strand and passing the end of the stringing material back through the loop. Pull on the end to tighten.

A *square knot* (figure 2) is made by forming an overhand knot with both ends of the stringing material, right end over left end. Repeat this, passing the left end over the right end to make the knot tight and secure.

A *surgeon's knot* (figure 3) is formed much like a square knot, but when tying the first overhand knot you make an additional wrap with the stringing material to secure the knot. Make a second overhand knot and pull to secure. This knot is very useful when you're trying to keep a tight tension on a difficult piece of beadwork.

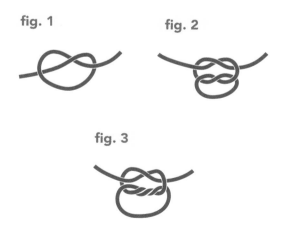

fig. 1   **fig. 2**

fig. 3

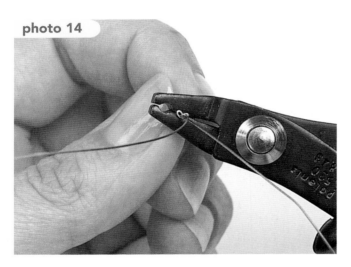

photo 14

Crimping

Crimping flexible beading wire is a fast and secure way to finish the ends of a piece of strung jewelry. I also like the way the tiny crimp beads blend with the overall design. You can flatten crimp beads and tubes with chain-nose pliers, but using crimping pliers (see page 20) is extra secure, and gives a clean, professional look.

1. String one crimp bead or crimp tube and the finding onto the beading wire. Pass the wire back through the crimp bead (but not the finding!) and pull to tighten.

2. Squeeze the crimp bead with the back opening on a pair of crimping pliers (photo 14).

3. Turn the crimp bead 90° and place it in the front opening of the pliers. Squeeze to form a nicely rounded bead (photo 15).

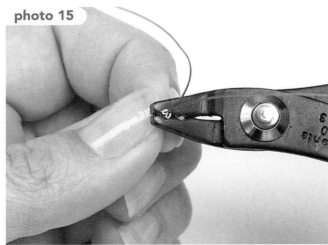

photo 15

Forming Filigree

Just about any flat filigree can be bent to a curve or folded shape. You'll find many examples in this book of how those beautiful flat pieces can become even lovelier with a bit of a bend. Bending filigree pieces allows you to create new shapes—you can curve a large, flat piece to create a cuff bracelet, or curl the points of a filigree flower into a setting for a stone. The metal will happily hold the shape you bend, so you can create forms that can be further adorned with beads, crystals or stones.

photo 16

photo 17

Curves

Many flat filigree pieces are available that would make perfect bracelets if they weren't so, well, flat. For a bracelet, a gentle curve enhances the comfort. I have bent large filigree pieces around just about anything that seems to have the right curve: a rolling pin, a table leg, a dowel rod or even a wooden spoon.

1. Hold the filigree against a rounded object.

2. Use your hands to press the filigreed piece into the shape as shown in photo 16. Check the shape periodically to make sure you don't over-bend the metal.

If you're curving several pieces of the same style filigree and each need to have identical bends, check the pieces against each other several times as you work. Try *spooning*, or stacking the pieces to test the shape.

Sharp bends

Making sharp bends in a piece of filigree completely changes the shape. You'll need to know how to make these bends when you create bezels, such as in the Carla necklace (page 98).

1. Determine the place you want to make the bends, possibly working from a sketch or photocopy of the piece of filigree. Place the filigree flat within the jaws of chain-nose pliers at the bend point.

2. Slowly and carefully make the bend (photo 17). Make many small adjustments rather than a few large ones, and take care to make any bend away from the front of the filigree. For multiple bends, work the filigree from side to side, not clockwise.

Changing Metal Finishes

While metal filigree is available in a variety of finishes, there are often times when you want to change the finish. Whether you want to mix various finishes in one piece of jewelry, subtly alter a plated finish, or dramatically change a plain finish, there are a variety of methods you can use to do this.

It's important to note that all heat-treating, sealing, or painting should take place before any beads are added to the filigree. Some treatments can harm the beads and the beads can get in the way of creating the desired finishes. Heat treatments especially can affect many types of beads causing them to crack, change color, or melt.

Before you change the finish on the filigree, determine if the metal is raw brass or plated. Raw brass will range in color from a bright and shiny yellow gold color to a dark, antique-looking patina. There will usually be some variation in the finish of raw brass and a darker color will rub off with a bit of baking soda and water. Plated finishes can be sterling silver, copper, or any other metal color, but will generally not rub off with baking soda. The easiest way to identify the finish is to ask about it when purchasing. When you return home, label the filigree before you store it.

Heat Treatments

Heat can be used to transform the finish on both raw and plated metals. Heat will darken bright yellow raw brass. It can remove the sealant coating on plated metal so you can paint it. Heat may darken the color, but will generally not remove a plated finish from metal.

You can apply heat to the filigree pieces in several ways. By using flame, either with a torch or your gas stove, you can remove the finish coating and do some subtle patinas. You can also use a heat gun designed for embossing or other paper arts. This method is ideal when you want to naturally darken or age raw brass filigree as seen in Coral Blossom (page 53) and Barcelona (page 39). Generally, heat guns will not burn off any surface coating or plating, but they will darken the metal. Filigree can also be heated using a butane torch. These torches get very hot (around 1300°F [704.4°C]) but with care you can use one safely in your home. The torch allows you to direct the heat to specific areas of the filigree to soften the metal or to create dark, aged areas. The directed flame is more efficient than a gas stove.

When creating a patina with flame, be careful when holding the filigree over a stove or other flame. Your tools will get quite hot! I use metal kitchen tongs for holding my filigree. To avoid contaminating food with any paints or patinas from the filigree I don't use the same tongs to cook my dinner. If you are heating sealed filigree to burn off a coating, please make sure you are working in a well ventilated area. Heating raw brass to patina the metal naturally, however, does not produce fumes.

To darken the metal with a heat gun:

1. Lay all the pieces you wish to darken on a heat-proof work surface. Make sure no pieces are touching.

2. Use the heat gun to gently warm the filigree pieces. As the color begins to change (within two to five minutes), watch the metal surface and pull the gun away as soon as the desired color is reached. If the surface is heating unevenly, move the gun around or rotate the piece with a pair of pliers or tongs. Be very careful as the metal will be quite hot.

3. After the pieces are cool, seal them with acrylic spray paint or allow the finish to wear naturally.

To darken the metal with a gas stove or torch:

1. Hold the filigree piece with tongs or pliers just over the flame. Make sure you move the metal around to create an even color and remove the metal from the flame as soon as the desired color is achieved.

2. After the pieces are cool, seal them with acrylic spray paint or allow the finish to wear naturally.

Sealants

Once you have heat-treated the surface of the metal you can allow it to continue to darken and age naturally or you can choose to seal it. A thin coating of *clear enamel spray paint* will seal the surface and keep the finish as-is for years. Another way to seal the finish is with *beeswax*. The coating traditionally used to seal a natural brass patina was beeswax, and it still works well. Beeswax is often sold at bead and sewing shops or you can try a local farmer's market or natural foods store. Rub a very small amount of beeswax onto a soft cloth and then rub the cloth onto the filigree. The metal finish will be a bit darker with the beeswax on the surface, and the soft patina will remain tarnish-free for a long time.

Paints

For a bit of whimsy, or just a different look, I love painted filigree. The color can make the lacy metal take on a whole new look, bright and cheery in primary colors, or dramatic and graphic in black or white. You can also use it to give an aged 'whitewashed' look, as in the Queen Anne's Lace necklace (page 90) or a verdigris patina as in the Verdi necklace (page 106).

My favorite paint for use on filigree is enamel spray paint. It comes in a wide variety of colors and is readily available at most paint or hardware stores. While you can't mix your own colors in the cans, layering different colors is possible. The thin coats you can make with spray paint create a durable finish that resists wear. Avoid spray paints that are latex or advertised as 'easy to clean up' or 'water washable.' They generally don't stick to the metal for very long.

Painting filigree is easy to do, but because you're painting on metal it's important to stick to these steps.

1. Clean the filigree by heat-treating it (see page 30). The heat helps remove any lacquer or burn off any processing oils, and ensures that the paint remains on the metal for years to come. After the cleaned filigree is cooled, handle it with gloves or tweezers so the oils from your hands don't cause the paint to flake later.

2. Choose a well-ventilated painting space, like a porch or garage, where the paint won't drift onto rugs or furniture.

3. Lay down a sheet or two of newsprint or scrap cardboard on the work surface. *Note:* I spray my pieces in a large shallow box about 6 inches (15.2 cm) deep. Use tweezers or wear gloves to place the filigree pieces on the paper.

4. Spray the front of the filigree with three light coats, allowing 60 to 90 minutes between coats. Flip the filigree over and paint the back in the same manner. Once the two sides have been painted, allow to dry overnight. Finish the piece with a single, thin coat of clear spray paint on each side and allow to dry for 24 hours.

You can also create a whitewashed or antiqued effect on filigree using just spray paint.

1. Clean the filigree by heat-treating it (page 30).

2. Apply a thin coat of clear spray paint.

3. While the clear coat is still quite wet, apply a thin coat of either white (for whitewash) or dark (for antique) paint. Use a smooth cotton rag to immediately wipe the surface of the filigree. This will remove the paint on the highest parts of the filigree design and leave paint in the open, lacy parts. *Note:* This is a tricky technique and you may want to practice it a few times until you get it right. You can repeat the painting and the wiping steps to make the effect more pronounced. This finish also works well on chain if you stick to working with short sections.

4. When you are pleased with the final look, allow the paint to dry overnight. Finish with a coat of clear spray paint and let dry.

PROJECTS

Red Lantern

These earrings want to boogie, but even if you're stuck behind a desk all day, the dagger drops will dance for you—*cha-cha-cha*—every time you move your head. Attaching the drops with jump rings lets them float freely.

Finished Size: 1½ inches (3.8 cm)

Materials

6 patinaed or raw brass filigree five-point bead caps, 6 mm

30 red glass dagger beads, 3 x 10 mm

10 red glass fire-polished beads, 4 mm

30 patinaed or raw brass jump rings, 4 mm

2 patinaed or raw brass head pins, 1 inch (2.5 cm)

1 pair of patinaed brass ear wires

Patinaed or raw brass 20-gauge wire, 6 inches (15.2 cm)

Clear acrylic spray paint or wax (optional)

Tools

Chain-nose pliers

Round-nose pliers

Wire cutters

Cookie sheet (optional)

Heat gun and heat-proof surface (optional)

Techniques

Opening and closing rings (page 25)

Simple loop (page 22)

Changing metal finish (page 30)

Instructions

1. If you can only find raw brass findings, patina them with a heat gun. Lay the wire, head pins, and jump rings on a cookie sheet and separate evenly. Set the cookie sheet on a heat-proof surface. Use a heat gun to apply heat to the findings until they darken. Keep an eye on the color and move the gun around to create an even finish. When all the findings are the preferred color, allow to cool. Seal the pieces with a clear finish coat, wax, or allow the pieces to continue to patina naturally.

2. Open a jump ring and slide on a glass dagger. Connect the ring to one of the openings at the edge of a bead cap (figure 1). Repeat around the bead cap to add five daggers in all. Set aside.

fig. 1

3. Repeat step 2 to make two more embellished caps.

4. Cut a 1½-inch (3.8 cm) length of wire. Form a simple loop at one end of the wire. Slide on one 4-mm bead and one embellished cap from outside to inside. Slip on one 4-mm bead so it nestles inside the embellished cap (figure 2). Form a simple loop to secure the cap and bead. Set aside.

fig. 2

5. Cut a 1½-inch (3.8 cm) length of wire. Form a simple loop at one end of the wire. Slide on one 4-mm bead and one embellished cap from inside to outside. Form a simple loop to secure the cap and bead.

6. Connect the cap links so the longer link attaches to the loop inside the shorter link (figure 3).

7. Slip one 4-mm bead onto a head pin. Slide on the remaining embellished cap from inside to outside. Add a 4-mm bead and form a simple loop to create a dangle.

fig. 3

8. Attach the dangle to the open loop of the longer cap link. Attach an ear wire to the remaining open cap link loop.

9. Repeat all steps to make a second earring.

Pavlova

Crystals sparkle against the filigree of this cuff. Pair it with a little black dress for a night on the town, or wear it as a lacy contrast to a black sweater and jeans during the day.

Finished size: Adjustable, up to 7
inches (17.8 cm)

Materials

3 gunmetal flat filigree squares, 42 mm

1 gunmetal teardrop filigree,
15 x 20 mm

32 light topaz crystal bicone beads,
4 mm

32 smoke metallic AB crystal round
beads, 3 mm

48 gunmetal head pins, 1 inch (2.5 cm)

48 antiqued brass 20-gauge head pins,
1 inch (2.5 cm)

36 antiqued brass 20-gauge oval jump
rings, or sturdy chain links, 5 x 7 mm

1 antiqued brass fish hook clasp,
19 mm

Tools

Rolling pin or wooden bracelet
mandrel

Round-nose pliers

Chain-nose pliers

Wire cutters

Techniques

Metal bending (page 29)

Opening and closing rings (page 25)

Simple loop (page 22)

Adding beads to filigree (page 26)

Instructions

1. Grasp a filigreed square so it sits right side up between the thumb and forefingers of each hand. Carefully bend an even, smooth curve (figure 1). Use a rolling pin or bracelet mandrel to refine the curve. Repeat for each square. Stack the squares to make sure their curves match and make adjustments as necessary. Set the squares aside.

fig. 1

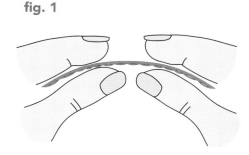

2. Look at the front of one of the squares. Note a circle made up of 16 filigree holes around the rosette pattern. Pass a brass head pin through one of the holes and trim the head pin to ⅜ inch (9 mm) (figure 2). Form a simple loop to secure the pin. Repeat around the circle to add 16 looped head pins in all. Repeat this step for each square.

fig. 2

fig. 3

fig. 4

3. Lay the three squares in a row, side by side. Use a round jump ring to connect the first two squares near the top and another round jump ring to connect the squares near the bottom. Repeat to connect the second and third squares (figure 3).

4. Attach an oval jump ring to a filigree hole at the center edge of the first square. Use another jump ring to connect the ring just placed to a third ring. Attach the clasp to the third ring (figure 4).

5. Attach an oval jump ring to a filigree hole at the center edge loop of the third square. Attach another jump ring to the one just placed. Continue to link oval jump rings to make a chain 14 rings long. Attach the filigreed teardrop to the last ring.

6. Slip a bead onto a gunmetal head pin. Form a simple loop to secure the bead. Repeat with all the beads to make 64 dangles in all.

7. Attach one topaz dangle to each brass loop on the first and third squares. Connect two smoke dangles to each brass loop on the second center square.

Barcelona

This necklace features a mix of contemporary and natural elements, and it is both ornate and modern. The interesting bail at the center of the pendant is made from a flat piece of filigree with a custom bend.

Barcelona

Finished size: 18 inches (45.7 cm)

Materials

1 antiqued brass filigree connector bar with two loops at each end, 10 x 30 mm

2 natural brass filigree bead caps, 12 mm

1 semiprecious labradorite stone oval bead, 16 x 22 mm

1 silver smoke crystal open square bead, 20 mm

15 gray freshwater pearls, 7 mm

1 bright hammered brass round ring, 33 mm

1 bright wavy brass round ring, 15 mm

5 natural brass oval decorative jump rings (from chain), 9 x 5 mm

2 antiqued brass head pins, 1 inch (2.5 cm)

1 antiqued brass spring ring clasp, 1 cm

4 x 5-mm natural brass rollo chain, 13½ inches (34.3 cm)

13-mm antiqued brass filed tube chain, 4½ inches (11.4 cm)

Gunmetal 22-gauge craft wire, 16 inches (40.6 cm)

Instructions

1. Cut the rollo chain into three pieces: one 5¼-inch (13.3 cm), one 4¼- inch (10.8 cm), and one 3½-inch (8.9 cm) length. Set aside.

2. Use chain-nose pliers to grasp the connector bar at its midpoint and make a 45° bend. Slide the connector bar through the open square to check the fit. Determine two even points on the bar to make bends that will accommodate both the crystal and the hammered ring. The end result will be a U shape. Use chain-nose pliers to make the bends (figure 1).

   fig. 1

3. Place the open square, corner side down, into the U shape. Place the hammered ring behind the open square.

4. Pass a head pin through a matching set of the bar's loops, from the open square side (front) to the ring side (back). Form a simple loop to secure the head pin. Repeat for the other set the bar's loops (figure 2). Set the pendant aside.

   fig. 2

5. Hold a bead cap in one hand as you press the end of the labradorite bead into it, allowing the cap to mold to the stone's shape. Repeat with the other cap.

6. Cut a 4-inch (10.2 cm) piece of wire and form a wrapped loop on one end. Slide on one bead cap from outside to inside the labradorite bead, and another bead cap from inside to outside. Form another wrapped loop to secure the beads. Set the labradorite link aside.

7. Cut a 4-inch (10.2 cm) piece of wire and form a wrapped loop on one end. Slip on five 7-mm beads and form another wrapped loop to secure the beads, creating the first pearl link. Cut another 4-inch (10.2 cm) piece of wire. Make a wrapped loop that attaches to an end loop of the first pearl link (figure 3).

   fig. 3

8. Slide on five 7-mm beads and form a wrapped loop to secure the beads. Cut a third 4-inch (10.2 cm) piece of wire and form a wrapped loop that attaches to the open loop at the end of the second pearl link. Slip on the remaining pearl beads and form a wrapped loop. Set the pearl link chain aside.

9. Use a decorative jump ring to connect the pendant's right-side simple loop to the wavy brass ring. Open another decorative jump ring and slip on the pendant's left-side simple loop, one end of the pearl link chain, one end of the tube chain, and one end of the 4¼-inch (10.8 cm) piece of rollo chain. Close the ring (figure 4).

fig. 4

10. Use a decorative jump ring to connect the open ends of the pearl link chain, the tube chain, and the 4¼-inch (10.8 cm) piece of rollo chain to the 3½-inch (8.9 cm) piece of rollo chain. Use chain-nose pliers to open a link at the other end of the 3½-inch (8.9 cm) rollo chain piece and attach it to the clasp. Close the link.

11. Use a decorative jump ring to connect the wavy brass ring to one end of the labradorite link. Use chain-nose pliers to open a link at the end of the 5¼-inch (13.3 cm) piece of rollo chain. Attach the link to the remaining loop on the labradorite link. Attach a decorative jump ring to the other end of the rollo chain.

Tools

Wire cutters

Chain-nose pliers

Round-nose pliers

Techniques

Opening and closing rings (page 25)

Simple loop (page 22)

Wrapped loop (page 24)

Forming filigree (page 28)

Pearl Pointe

This ring might give you a sudden urge to gesture more while you talk. The head pin rivets used on the inside of the filigree dome are the secret ingredients in allowing the crystals and pearls to stand up and dance.

Finished size: 2 cm ring top

Materials

1 gold-plated filigree dome, 20 mm

7 light topaz AB crystal round beads, 4 mm

7 white keishi pearls, 6 mm

7 clear seed beads, size 10° or 11°

7 gold-filled regular head pins, 1 inch (2.5 cm)

7 gold-filled 22-gauge head pins with ball end, 1 inch (2.5 cm)

1 gold-plated square-top screen ring finding (ring base only), 20 mm

Tools

Chain-nose pliers

Round-nose pliers

Wire cutters

Techniques

Simple loop (page 22)

Wrapped loop (page 24)

Bending filigree (page 29)

Instructions

1. Slip a seed bead on a regular head pin and pass the head pin through one of the dome's holes from inside to outside. Slide on a crystal bead and form a wrapped loop to secure the beads (figure 1). Repeat to fill each of the seven holes at the top of the dome. Set aside.

fig. 1

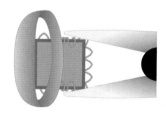

2. Slide a pearl onto a ball-end head pin. Form a wrapped loop that attaches to one of the wrapped loops already placed on the dome (figure 2). Repeat around to place all the pearls.

fig. 2

3. Note the 14 filigreed points on the outside edge of the dome's shape. Place the dome on top of the ring base and choose the four points that match best with the ring base's corners. Use chain-nose pliers to bend each of the four points outward at 90° angles (figure 3).

fig. 3

4. Place the dome on top of the ring base. Note the non-bent filigreed points that lay on the left and right sides of the ring. Use chain-nose pliers to carefully squeeze these points down along the sides and underneath the ring base to make a snug fit (figure 4). Don't bend the points at the corners or at the top and bottom of the ring.

fig. 4

An alternate version

Flora

If you can't decide which treasured photo to cradle in this elegant locket, insert a favorite quote instead, or even the definition of a special word cut from a vintage dictionary.

Finished size: Adjustable,
up to 18 inches (45.7 cm)

Materials

Antiqued brass oval filigree locket, 32 mm

21 white glass pearls, 8 mm

26 brass crimp beads, 2 mm

1 brass square jump ring, ¾ inch (1.9 cm)

1 antiqued brass fishhook clasp, 17 mm

1 antiqued brass five-petal bead cone,
4 x 6 mm

1 antiqued brass head pin, 1 inch (2.5 cm)

5-mm antiqued brass chain, 12 inches
(30.5 cm)

Medium-width flexible beading wire,
12 inches (30.5 cm)

Tools

Chain-nose or crimping pliers

Measuring tape

Wire cutters

Round-nose pliers

Techniques

Crimping (page 28)

Opening and closing loops (page 25)

Simple loops (page 22)

Instructions

1. Slip one pearl and the petal cone onto a head pin. Form a simple loop to secure the beads. Set the dangle aside.

2. String 13 crimp beads onto the beading wire, leaving a 1-inch (2.5 cm) tail. Pass the wire back through the first bead strung and snug the beads. Use chain-nose pliers to squeeze the crimp just exited. String on 20 pearls and 13 crimp beads. Pass back through the first crimp bead strung, snug the beads, and crimp (figure 1).

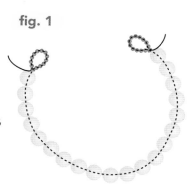

fig. 1

3. Gently open the jump ring and attach it to the ring at the top of the locket. Lay the strand of pearls inside the jump ring between the tenth and eleventh pearls. Close the ring.

4. Cut the chain into one 5-inch (12.7 cm) and one 8-inch (20.3 cm) length. Open a chain link at one end of the shorter chain and attach it to the loop on one side of the pearl strand. Repeat to add the longer chain to the other end of the pearl strand.

fig. 2

5. Connect the clasp to the open end of the shorter chain. Attach the pearl dangle to the open end of the longer chain (figure 2).

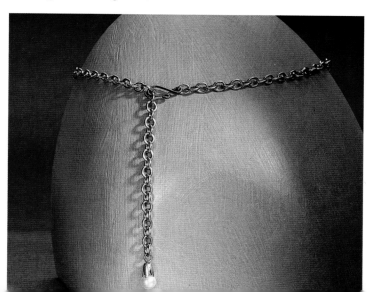

Trillium

These earrings feature tiny freshwater pearls and leave a bit of the delicate filigree exposed. Wear them when getting a latté with a friend or for a special night out.

Finished size: 1½ inches (3.8 cm)

Materials

2 antiqued brass dapped six-point filigree flowers, 20 mm

2 antiqued brass flat six-point filigree flowers, 20 mm

2 peacock iris freshwater pearl beads, 7 mm

2 lavender iris freshwater pearl beads, 7 mm

48 iris freshwater pearl beads, 2 mm

6 antiqued brass oval jump rings, 4 x 5 mm

1 pair of antiqued brass lever-back ear wires

Medium-width flexible beading wire, 48 inches (1.2 m)

Gunmetal 22-gauge craft wire, 3 inches (7.6 cm)

Tools

Wire cutters

Chain-nose pliers

Round-nose pliers

Techniques

Sewing beads to filigree (page 26)

Knotting (page 27)

Opening and closing rings (page 25)

Instructions

1. Cut a 24-inch (61 cm) length of flexible wire. Set aside.

2. Cut the 22-gauge wire into two 1½-inch (3.8 cm) pieces. Set aside.

3. Use one of the flexible wire lengths to string on a 7-mm bead. Sew the bead to the center of one of the dapped flowers, leaving a 4-inch (10.2 cm) tail. Tie the ends into a tight square knot at the back of the flower. Don't trim the ends

4. Pass the flexible wire up through the flower to exit from a filigree hole at the base of a petal. String on four 2-mm beads and pass down through the petal's point, opposite from where you exited. Pass up through the hole on the other side of the petal point, string on four more 2-mm beads, and pass down through the filigree at the base of the petal. Skip a filigree petal and pass up through the base of the next petal (figure 1). Repeat this step twice to add beads to the third and fifth petals.

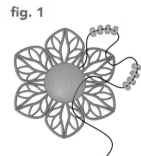

fig. 1

5. Stack the beaded flower with a flat flower, backs touching and petals aligned. Use jump rings to connect the unbeaded petal points to their flat filigree mates. Set aside.

6. Form a simple loop at one end of one of the pieces. Slip on one 7-mm bead and form another simple loop to secure the bead. Set the link aside.

7. Connect the one end of the link to a jump ring on the flower (figure 2). Connect the other end of the link to an ear wire.

fig. 2

8. Repeat steps 3 through 7 to make a second earring.

Dinner at Eight

This necklace pairs diamond-shaped filigree connectors with sparkly crystal beads that have a similar profile. The result is a balanced yet asymmetrical piece that's perfect for a night out on the town.

Materials

Finished size: 24 inches (61 cm)

10 gold-plated diamond-shaped two-loop flat filigree connectors, 45 mm long

2 peach crystal bicone beads, 8 mm

10 peach crystal bicone beads, 6 mm

6 gold-filled jump rings, 8 mm

7-mm link gold-filled chain, 30 inches (76.2 cm)

Gold-filled 20-gauge wire, 15 inches (38.1 cm)

Tools

Wire cutters

Round-nose pliers

Chain-nose pliers

Techniques

Simple loops (page 22)

Working with jump rings (page 25)

Metal forming (page 29)

Instructions

1. Cut the chain into three separate pieces: one 2½-inch (6.4 cm), one 5-inch (12.7 cm), and one 21½-inch length (54.6 cm). Set aside.

2. Cut a 1-inch (2.5 cm) piece of wire and form a simple loop at one end. Slip on one 6-mm bead and form another simple loop to secure the bead. Repeat for each 6-mm crystal to make ten small bead links in all. Cut two 1¼-inch (3.2 cm) lengths of wire and use 8-mm beads to make two large bead links in the same manner. Set all the links aside.

3. Use chain-nose pliers to create a slight bend along the short center line of each piece of filigree, angling the bend away from the front (figure 1). Examine all the pieces to make sure they are bent at the same angle. Test this by stacking the pieces on top of each other. Adjust the pieces that don't match up.

fig. 1

fig. 2

4. Place two filigree pieces back to back. Attach one end of a small link to the stacked filigrees' loops. Use another small link to connect the loops at the other end of the filigree pair (figure 2). Set aside. Repeat for all of the filigree pairs to make ten short filigree sections.

5. Attach one large link to one end of a short filigree section. Attach another short filigree section. Repeat on the other end of the same filigree pair to make a long filigree section (figure 3).

fig. 3

6. Use jump rings to connect the filigree sections to the chain lengths in this sequence: the long filigree section, the 5-inch (12.7 cm) chain piece, one short filigree section, the 2½-inch (6.4 cm) chain piece, one short filigree section, and the 21½-inch (54.6 cm) chain piece. Use the last jump ring to connect the end of the long chain to the open end of the long filigree section.

Whirlwind

Bright and whimsical, these cheery earrings mix painted filigree with silk ribbon for a pop of color. Wear them on a spring day and get whirled away.

Finished size: 1½ inches (3.8 cm)

Materials

2 raw brass filigree pinwheels, 48 mm

2 aqua crystal bicone beads, 8 mm

40 turquoise fire-polished glass round beads, 4 mm

1 pair of sterling silver ear wires

Thin-width silver-toned flexible beading wire, 24 inches (61 cm)

Sterling silver 20-gauge wire, 2 inches (5.1 cm)

Turquoise silk 4-mm embroidery ribbon, 16 inches (40.6 cm)

Jadite green enamel spray paint

Clear enamel spray paint

Newsprint or scrap cardboard

Tools

Wire cutters

Scissors

Chain-nose pliers

Round-nose pliers

Techniques

Changing the finish of filigree (page 30)

Knotting (page 27)

Simple loop (page 22)

Sewing beads to filigree (page 26)

Opening and closing rings (page 25)

Instructions

1. Cut the flexible wire into two 12-inch (30.5 cm) lengths. Set aside.

2. Cut the sterling silver wire into two 1-inch (2.5 cm) pieces. Set aside.

3. Cut the ribbon into two 8-inch (20.3 cm) lengths. Set aside.

4. Heat-treat the pinwheels and clean them so they're free of lint or dust. Set aside.

5. Working in a well-ventilated area, set a few sheets of newsprint or scrap cardboard down to protect your work surface. Lay the pinwheels faceup on the work surface and use green paint to spray a thin coat on the front of the pinwheels. Allow them to dry for at least two hours. Spray on a second coat and let the pinwheels dry again. Flip the pinwheels over and spray the back sides, allowing them to dry for two hours. Turn the pinwheels over and spray on a thin, clear coat of enamel; allow to dry for at least two hours. Spray another clear coat on the front, and at least one more on the back. Allow the finished pieces to dry for 24 hours so the paint can cure. Set the pinwheels aside.

6. Pass one end of the ribbon up through the edge of one of the pinwheels, leaving a 4-inch (10.2 cm) tail. Wrap the ribbon around the pinwheel's edge and pass up through the next hole in the filigree (figure 1). Repeat around to completely embellish the pinwheel's edge with ribbon. Tie a square knot with the ribbon ends and trim.

fig. 1

fig. 2

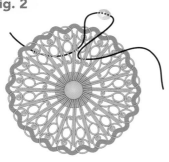

7. Pass one of the flexible wire lengths up through the pinwheel where indicated in figure 2. String on one 4-mm bead and pass down through the filigree to seat the bead. Pass up through the filigree's next hole and add another 4-mm bead. Continue around the circle to add 20 beads in all. Use the wire ends to tie a square knot on the back of the filigree and trim the ends. Set the pinwheel aside.

8. Form a simple loop at the end of one of the sterling silver wire pieces. Slide on one 8-mm bead and form another simple loop to secure the bead. Attach one of the bead link loops to an ear wire. Attach the other end of the bead link to the top of the pinwheel.

9. Repeat steps 6 through 8 to make a second earring.

Coral Blossom

Slip on this set, and suddenly you're transported to the Orient. The warm color of the beads conjures the heady aroma of spices in a souk, and the lacy filigree brings to mind ornate palace architecture.

Coral Blossom

Finished size: 18 inches (45.7 cm)

Materials

Necklace:

2 natural brass six-petal dapped filigree flowers, 40 mm

4 natural brass filigree bead caps, 7 x 9 mm

3 faceted round carnelian beads, 8 mm

10 red branch coral nugget beads, 6 mm

108 red branch coral nugget beads, 2 mm

10 oval natural brass decorative jump rings, 6 x 10 mm

4 natural brass jump rings, 5 mm

1 natural brass hook-and-eye clasp, 18 mm

4 x 5-mm link antiqued brass chain, 8 inches (20.3 cm)

Gunmetal 20-gauge craft wire, 16 inches (40.6 cm)

Brass-tone fine-width flexible beading wire, 2 yards (1.8 m)

Earrings:

6 natural brass filigree leaves, 8 mm

2 red branch coral nugget beads, 6 mm

6 red branch coral nugget beads, 2 mm

6 natural brass head pins, 1 inch (2.5 cm)

6 oval natural brass decorative jump rings, 6 x 10 mm

2 antiqued brass ear wires

Gunmetal 20-gauge wire, 2 inches (5.1 cm)

Instructions

Necklace

1. Cut a 6-inch (15.2 cm) length of flexible wire. String on an 8-mm bead and set it on the top center of the filigree flower. Pass the wire ends down through the filigree. Tie a knot to secure the bead (figure 1).

fig. 1

2. Cut a 12-inch (30.5 cm) length of flexible wire. Tie the wire to the base of one of the petals, leaving a 4-inch (10.2 cm) tail. The knot should sit at the back of the filigree. Pass the longer wire end up through the filigree. String on two 2-mm beads, stretch the strand across the base of the petal, and pass down through the filigree. Stretch the wire across the back of the petal and pass up through the filigree so it exits just above the first bead strung in the previous row (figure 2).

fig. 2

Repeat, stitching 2-mm beads to the petal in parallel rows. Bead a total of five rows, the next with three beads, the following with four, then five, and finally, four. Weave the wire back through the filigree and tie the working wire to the tail.

Repeat this step until all the petals are beaded. Trim any excess wire. Set aside.

fig. 3

3. Cut the chain into two 4-inch (10.2 cm) pieces. Set aside.

4. Stack the beaded and plain filigree flowers so the curved sides face outward. Use 5-mm jump rings to connect four pairs of petal tips as shown in figure 3.

Tools

Wire cutters

Chain-nose pliers

Round-nose pliers

Techniques

Knotting (page 27)

Opening and closing rings (page 25)

Simple loop (page 22)

Sewing beads to filigree (page 26)

5. Cut a 3-inch (7.6 cm) length of gunmetal wire and form a simple loop at one end. Thread on one bead cap from outside to inside, one 8-mm bead, and one bead cap from inside to outside. Form another simple loop to secure the caps and bead. Repeat to make a second large bead link. Set aside.

6. Cut a 1-inch (2.5 cm) length of gunmetal wire and form a simple loop at one end. Slip on one 6-mm bead and form another simple loop to secure the bead. Repeat with the remaining 6-mm beads. Set the small bead links aside.

7. Use one decorative jump ring to connect one of the jump rings attached to the filigree flower to the end of a large bead link. Use another decorative jump ring to attach the other end of the large bead link to a small bead link. Continue the chain by alternately connecting decorative jump rings with small bead links until you've used five small bead links in all. Attach the last bead link to the end of one chain length. Add one half of the clasp to the open end of the chain.

8. Repeat step 7 to create the other side of the necklace.

Earrings

1. Slide one 2-mm bead onto a head pin. Form a simple loop to secure the bead. Repeat twice. Set the bead dangles aside.

2. Cut a 1-inch (2.5 mm) length of wire and form a simple loop at one end. Slip on one 6-mm bead and form another simple loop to secure the bead link.

3. Connect one end of one of the bead links to an ear wire. Set aside.

4. Open a decorative jump ring and slide on one filigree leaf and one bead dangle. Close the ring. Open a second ring, slide on one filigree leaf, one bead dangle, and the first ring. Close the ring. Open a third ring, slide on one filigree leaf, one bead dangle, and the second ring. Close the ring (figure 4).

fig. 4

5. Connect one end of the embellished chain made in the previous step to the open end of the bead link.

6. Repeat steps 1 through 5 to make a second earring.

Byzantine

With a mix of glass and jasper beads, filigree bead caps, and cones, this lariat and earrings set is the perfect accent to a casual outfit. The square jump rings offset the elaborate filigree.

Materials

Earrings

4 antiqued copper filigree bead caps, 8 mm

2 terra cotta fire-polished beads, 12 mm

2 antiqued copper square jump rings, ½ inch (1.3 cm)

2 antiqued copper 20-gauge head pins, 2 inches (5.1 cm)

2 antiqued copper lever-back earring findings

Lariat

2 antiqued copper filigree bead caps, 8 mm

2 faceted round white jasper beads, 20 mm

2 terra cotta fire-polished beads, 12 mm

2 antiqued copper bead cones, 14 mm x 22 mm

2 antiqued copper square jump rings, ½ inch (1.3 cm)

2 antiqued copper 20-gauge head pins, 2 inches (5.1 cm)

5 x 6-mm oval antiqued copper chain, 18 inches (45.7 cm)

Antiqued copper 20-gauge wire, 6 inches (15.2 cm)

Instructions

Earrings

1. Slide one bead cap onto a head pin from outside to inside. Slip on one 12-mm bead and one bead cap from inside to outside (figure 1). Form a simple loop to secure the caps and bead. Set the dangle aside.

fig. 1

2. Use one jump ring to attach the dangle to the earring finding.

3. Repeat steps 1 and 2 to make a second earring.

Tools

Chain-nose pliers

Round-nose pliers

Wire cutters

Techniques

Opening and closing rings (page 25)

Simple loop (page 22)

Lariat

1. Slide one bead cap onto a head pin from outside to inside. Slip on one 20-mm jasper bead and use your fingers to press the bead down onto the cap to spread the cap outward until it fits the bead's shape. Slide on one cone from inside to outside. Form a simple loop to secure the cap, bead, and cone. Repeat this step to make a second jasper dangle. Set aside.

2. Cut the wire in two 3-inch (7.6 cm) pieces. Make a simple loop on one end of one of the wires. Slide one bead cap onto the wire from outside to inside. Slip on one 12-mm bead and one bead cap from inside to outside. Form a simple loop to secure the caps and bead. Repeat to make a second bead link. Set aside.

3. Use a jump ring to connect one bead link with one jasper dangle (figure 2).

4. Connect one end of the chain to the bead link (figure 3). Repeat at the other end of the chain. ***Note:*** If desired, make a traditional necklace, or "faux lariat" by connecting the two jump rings; cut the chain in half and add a clasp.

fig. 2

fig. 3

The tiny crystals on these shimmery earrings capture and refract the light. Wear these accent pieces with a white shirt and jeans and let them draw all eyes to you.

Finished size: 2½ inches (6.7 cm)

Materials

9 gold-plated filigree teardrops, 15 x 20 mm

36 clear AB crystal bicone beads, 2 mm

22 gold-filled head pins, 1 inch (2.5 cm)

1 pair of gold-filled 24-gauge ear wires

Gold-filled 24-gauge wire, 6 inches (15.2 cm)

Tools

Chain-nose pliers

Round-nose pliers

Wire cutters

Techniques

Simple loop (page 22)

Opening and closing rings (page 25)

Instructions

1. Slide one bead onto a head pin and form a simple loop to secure it. ***Note:*** It may help to very gently grasp the crystal with chain-nose pliers while turning the loop with round-nose pliers. Repeat to make 11 dangles in all. Set aside.

2. Cut a 1-inch (2.5 cm) length of wire. Form a simple loop at one end. Slide on one bead and form a simple loop to secure it. Repeat to make six bead links in all. Set aside.

3. Use your fingers to shape one of the ear wires until it's a smooth curve. Slide on one bead and use your fingers to reshape the ear wire.

4. Lay the teardrops, faceup, in three rows: one in row 1, three in row 2, and three in row 3.

fig. 1

5. Attach the ear wire to the top of the row 1 teardrop. Use a bead link to connect the top of the first row 2 teardrop to the bottom left hole of the row 1 teardrop; a link to connect the top of the second row 2 teardrop to the bottom center hole of the row 1 teardrop; and a third link to connect the top of the third row 2 teardrop to the bottom right hole of the row 1 teardrop. Use bead links to connect the top of each row 3 teardrop to the bottom center hole of each row 2 teardrop (figure 1).

fig. 2

6. Add one dangle to each of the three holes at the bottom of the row 3 teardrops. Connect one dangle to the bottom left hole of the first row 1 teardrop, and one to the bottom right hole of the third row 1 tear drop (figure 2).

7. Repeat all steps to make a second earring.

Susan

She's the buttoned-up type, shirt always pressed. Wears a pearly pin that could have been her mother's. But at night, she takes that same pin, attaches it to the décolletage of a teensy black dress, and goes from demure to daring.

Finished size: 2 inches (5.1 cm)

Materials

1 natural brass dapped filigree square rosette, 50 mm

18 white freshwater pearl round beads, 5 mm

28 peach freshwater pearl round beads, 5 mm

51 clear AB seed beads, size 10° or 11°

3 clear AB crystal bicone beads, 3 mm (or 3 seed beads)

1 antiqued brass brooch set, backing only, 1¼ inch

Fine-width flexible beading wire, 72 inches (1.8 m)

Strong, clear adhesive glue

Tools

Wire cutters

Chain-nose pliers

Techniques

Knotting (page 27)

Sewing beads to filigree (page 26)

Instructions

1. Cut the beading wire into three 12-inch (30.5 cm) lengths and one 36-inch (91.4 cm) length. Set aside.

2. String eight pearl beads on one 12-inch (30.5 cm) wire, alternating peach and white. Leaving a 4-inch (10.2 cm) tail, tie a square knot to form a tight circle of beads. Don't trim.

3. Place the bead circle on the center front of the rosette and pass the wire ends down through the filigree. Pass the long wire end back up through the filigree between the next two beads in the circle. Cross over the wire between beads and pass back down through the filigree (figure 1). Continue in this manner to completely sew the circle to the rosette. Use the working and tail wires to tie a tight square knot. Trim the wire ends.

4. String 14 white pearl beads on the next 12-inch (30.5 cm) wire. Fit this circle around the beads already attached to the pin to check for fit. Leaving a 4-inch (10.2 cm) tail, tie a square knot to form a tight circle of beads. Don't trim.

fig. 1

5. Place the bead circle around the circle already affixed to the rosette. Repeat step 3 to sew this bead circle to the filigree.

6. String 21 peach pearl beads on the final 12-inch (30.5 cm) wire. Leaving a 4-inch (10.2 cm) tail, tie a square knot to form a tight circle of beads. Don't trim.

7. Place the bead circle around the circles already affixed to the rosette. Repeat step 3 to sew this bead circle to the filigree (figure 2).

fig. 2

8. Pass the ends of the 36-inch (91.4 cm) wire up through the center of the filigree and tie a square knot to secure. Use one wire end to string on 17 seed beads, one peach pearl bead, and one bicone bead. Pass back through the pearl bead just strung and down through the filigree. Tie a square knot to secure the beads. Repeat to create three fringe legs (figure 3). Don't trim the wire. ***Note:*** You may need to switch to the other wire end to create the last fringe leg. Just be sure to leave at least a 4-inch (10.2 cm) tail on either wire.

fig. 3

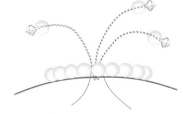

9. Twist the three fringe legs together to form a coil. Pass the remaining end of the wire up through the center of the rosette. Sew the beads at the end of the fringe legs to the center of the rosette to hold the coil in place. Pass down through the filigree, use the wire ends to make a tight square knot, and trim (figure 4).

fig. 4

10. Trim the prongs off the pin back. Place a dab of glue in the center of the pin back and press it onto the back of the filigree. Allow it to dry 24 hours before wearing.

Parisienne

Wear this sparkling ensemble, and *voilà!* You are suddenly an elegant mademoiselle strolling along the Champs-Elysées. Both parts of the set are simple pieces to make, but no one will know you didn't buy it from a fine Paris *bijouterie*. They'll just be thinking "ooh la la."

Finished size: necklace, 30 inches (76.2 cm); earrings, 1½ inches (3.8 cm)

Materials

Necklace

132 shiny brass filigree bead caps, 8 mm

66 mottled rose fire-polished round beads, 10 mm

67 rose fire-polished rondelles, 4 mm

1 gold-filled 20-gauge head pin, 2 inches (5.1 cm)

1 gold-filled split or soldered ring, 9 mm

2 gold-filled jump rings, 8 mm

2 gold-filled crimp beads, 2 x 2 mm

2 gold-filled crimp covers, 4 mm

1 gold-filled lobster clasp, 12 mm

Medium-width flexible beading wire, 38 inches (96.5 cm)

Earrings

6 gold-filled filigree bead caps, 8 mm

2 mottled rose fire-polished round beads, 10 mm

2 rose fire-polished rondelles, 4 mm

10 caramel-swirled fire-polished round beads, 6 mm

10 pink seed beads, size 11°

2 gold-filled 20-gauge head pins, 2 inches (5.1 cm)

10 gold-filled 20-gauge head pins, 1 inch (2.5 cm)

1 pair of gold-filled ear wires

Gold-filled 20-gauge wire , 4 inches (10.2 cm)

Instructions

Necklace

1. Slide a bead cap, outside to inside, onto a head pin. Slip on one 10-mm bead and a bead cap, inside to outside. Form a simple loop to secure the caps and bead. Attach the dangle to the split ring (figure 1).

fig. 1

2. Use a crimp bead to attach one end of the flexible wire to the split ring. String on one gold-filled bead. String on a sequence of one rondelle, one bead cap from outside to inside, one 10-mm bead, and one bead cap from inside to outside. Repeat the sequence 64 times. String on one rondelle, one gold-filled bead, one crimp tube, and the clasp. Pass back through the crimp tube, snug the beads, and crimp.

3. Add a crimp cover to each crimp bead.

Earrings

1. Slip one pink seed bead and one 6-mm bead onto a 1-inch (2.5 cm) head pin. Form a simple loop to secure the beads. Repeat to make five dangles in all. Set aside.

2. Attach one dangle to each of the five openings at the edge of a bead cap (figure 2).

3. Slide one rondelle on a 2-inch (5.1 cm) head pin. Slip the embellished bead cap onto the head pin from inside to outside, another bead cap from outside to inside, one 10-mm bead, and one bead cap from inside to outside (figure 3). Form a simple loop to secure the caps and beads. Connect the loop to an ear wire.

4. Repeat all steps to make a second earring.

fig. 2

fig. 3

Snowflake

This ethereal bracelet is lightweight, allowing it to drift like a winter breeze across the wrist. Delicate pearls are nestled in and below the filigree and seem to float, light as a cloud, surrounded by the organza bow closure.

Finished size: 6 inches (15.2 cm);
adjusts infinitely with ribbon ties

Materials

8 sterling silver-plated ten-point filigree snowflakes with sunken center, 16 mm

32 white freshwater pearl beads, 5 mm

24 sterling silver head pins, 1 inch (2.5 cm)

14 sterling silver oval jump rings, 3 x 4 mm

4 sterling silver round jump rings, 5 mm

2 sterling silver fold-over ribbon end crimps, 5 x 8 mm

Fine-width sterling silver-coated flexible beading wire, 64 inches (1.6 m)

1-inch (2.5-cm) pearl white organza ribbon, 2 yards

Tools

Scissors

Wire cutters

Round-nose pliers

Chain-nose pliers

Techniques

Opening and closing rings (page 25)

Simple loop (page 22)

Sewing beads to filigree (page 26)

Instructions

1. Cut the ribbon into two 1-yard (0.9 m) lengths. Set aside.

2. Cut the beading wire into eight 8-inch (20.3 cm) lengths. Set aside.

3. Pass the ends of a length of beading wire through a snowflake from back to front. The ends should exit on each side of the center (figure 1). String a bead on one wire end and tie a tight square knot. The knot should sit close to the bead and be somewhat hidden. Trim the wire ends. Repeat to create eight beaded snowflakes in all.

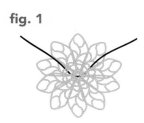

fig. 1

4. Lay the snowflakes side by side so two points of one snowflake touch two points of the next one. Use oval jump rings to connect the adjacent points, creating a chain of eight snowflakes. Attach round jump rings to the two points at each end of the chain (figure 2). Set aside.

fig. 2

5. Slip one bead onto a head pin. Form a simple loop to secure the bead. Repeat to make 24 dangles in all. Set aside.

6. Attach one dangle to the first snowflake's point closest to a jump ring. Attach another dangle to the adjacent point, and another to a third so there are three dangles on one side of the bracelet (figure 3). Repeat across, attaching three dangles to each snowflake. All the dangles should sit on the same side of the chain.

fig. 3

7. Attach an end crimp to the round jump rings at one end of the chain. Repeat at the other end of the chain. Set aside.

8. Fold one of the ribbon lengths in half and twist it at the center mark to temporarily make it thinner. Loop the ribbon through the end crimp, around the ring on the end of the finding, and back through the crimp (figure 4). The ribbon ends should be more or less the same length, but they don't have to be exact. Use chain-nose pliers to gently press the sides of the end crimp in to hold the ribbon in place. Press one side of the end crimp very flat before starting the second side. Even if a small amount of ribbon protrudes, it will still be quite secure.

9. Repeat step 8 at the other end of the chain.

10. Trim the ribbon ends to 45° angles. To wear, tie the bracelet to your wrist.

fig. 4

Lucille

Colorful and fun, this necklace is off-balance and quirky. The mixed beads and asymmetrical filigree look random, but they're carefully balanced to hang evenly on your neck.

Finished size: 24 inches (60 cm)

Materials

3 raw brass filigree pinwheels, 48 mm

97 assorted red glass beads,
3 to 9 mm

27 antiqued brass 20-gauge head
pins, 1 inch (2.5 cm)

5 x 6-mm antiqued brass chain,
34 inches (86.4 cm)

Gunmetal 20-gauge craft wire,
10 inches (25.4 cm)

Bright red enamel spray paint

Clear enamel spray paint

Newsprint or scrap cardboard

Tools

Wire cutters

Chain-nose pliers

Round-nose pliers

Techniques

Changing the filigree finish (page 30)

Opening and closing rings (page 25)

Simple loop (page 22)

Note

The project shown was created
using many vintage beads, so
it may be impossible to make
an exact duplicate. Instead, use
orphan beads from your bead
stash in your favorite color and
work with them. Paint the filigree
to match your beads.

Instructions

1. Cut the chain into three pieces: one 9-inch (22.9 cm), one 11-inch (27.9 cm), and one 14-inch (35.6 cm) length. Set aside.

2. Clean the pinwheels so they're free of lint or dust. Set aside.

3. Working in a well-ventilated area, set a few sheets of newsprint or scrap cardboard down to protect your work surface. Use red paint to spray a thin coat on the front of the pinwheels. Allow to dry for 60 to 90 minutes. Spray on a second coat and let dry again. Flip the pinwheels over and spray the back sides, allowing to dry for 60 to 90 minutes. Turn the pinwheels over and spray a thin, clear coat of enamel; allow to dry for at least 60 to 90 minutes. Spray another clear coat on the front, and at least one on the back. Allow the finished pieces to dry for 24 hours so the paint can cure.

4. Lay out the necklace design. Start by placing the pinwheels so there are two pieces on the left side and one piece on the right. Lay the chain pieces so the 11-inch (27.9 cm) length is at the top of the necklace, the 14-inch (35.6 cm) length is at the bottom, and the 9-inch (22.9-cm) length crosses between the top two pinwheels (figure 1).

fig. 1

5. Spend some time with the accent beads, experimenting with placement. The beads will attach to the chain in dangles, so group the smaller beads in sets to create longer dangles, and let the larger beads stand on their own. Always keep the balance of bead color and size in mind. Place about two-thirds of the beads on the left side of the necklace, the remaining beads mainly on the right side. Set aside some beads to connect the pinwheels to the chains.

6. Cut a length of wire as long as your bead, or bead set, plus ¾ inch (1.9 cm). Form a simple loop at one end, slip on the bead(s) and form another simple loop to secure. Repeat to make at least seven bead links of different sizes.

7. Imagine the pinwheel on the right side of the necklace as a clock face. Connect bead links to the pinwheel: one at twelve o'clock, one at five o'clock, and one at seven o'clock.

8. Repeat the placement in step 7 for the top pinwheel on the left side of the necklace, this time adding two links to the seven o'clock position. Connect the two pinwheels on the necklace's left side with the seven o'clock links. Attach two links to the bottom pinwheel's six o'clock position (figure 2).

9. Use the bead links at the top left and top right of the pinwheels to attach the 14-inch (35.6 cm) piece of chain. Use the bead link at the bottom left pinwheel's five o'clock position to attach the 11-inch (27.9 cm) piece of chain to the right-side pinwheel's seven o'clock position.

10. Use the remaining attached bead links to add the 9-inch (22.9 cm) piece of chain across the middle of the necklace.

11. Slide the remaining beads onto head pins, singly or in groups of two to five. Secure the beads with a simple loop to make dangles. Attach the dangles to the 11-inch (27.9 cm) and 9-inch (22.9 cm) chain links, as shown in figure 3. Spend some time balancing the dangles as you work, noting the weight and size of the various beads and placing them in their best positions. The dangle placement is not only aesthetic, it is necessary to keep the necklace weighted properly.

12. Try on the necklace to see if you are pleased with the design. If necessary, move the dangles until you achieve the desired effect.

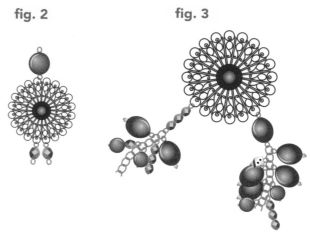

fig. 2   fig. 3

Twinkling Leaf

This lovely earring design combines natural brass filigree with green garnet, clear quartz, and green crystal. The brass and beads chime as you wear these earrings, evoking an enchanted glade with a hint of sparkle—is that a garden sprite peeking out of its golden cage?

Finished size: 1½ inches (3.8 cm)

Materials

2 natural brass four-petal filigree bead caps, 12 mm

4 natural brass filigree bead caps, 8 mm

8 natural brass filigree leaves, 5 x 7 mm

2 green garnet rondelle beads, 10 mm

2 crystal quartz rondelle beads, 8 mm

2 tourmaline green crystal round beads, 4 mm

2 copper head pins, 2 inches (5.1 cm)

8 natural brass round jump rings, 5 mm

2 natural brass oval decorative jump rings (from chain), 5 x 10 mm

1 pair of copper ear wires

Tools

Round-nose pliers

Wire cutters

Chain-nose pliers

Techniques

Simple loop (page 22)

Opening and closing rings (page 25)

Instructions

1. Slip one petal bead cap, outside to inside, onto a head pin. Add one 10-mm bead and use your fingers to gently press the bead into the cap so the curves match. Slide on one bead cap from inside to outside and form a simple loop to secure the caps and bead (figure 1). Keep the trimmed end handy. Set the dangle aside.

fig. 1

fig. 2

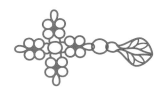

2. Use a round jump ring to connect one leaf to the hole on one of the points of a filigree bead cap (figure 2). Make sure that the leaf faces outward. Repeat on each point of the cap.

3. Form a simple loop at the end of the leftover wire from step 1. Slip on one 8-mm bead, one 4-mm bead, and a four-petal bead cap from inside to outside. The beads should nestle within the cap. Form a simple loop to secure the beads and cap. Set the beaded link aside.

4. Use chain-nose pliers to gently open an oval jump ring. Slide on the dangle and beaded link and close the ring.

5. Add an ear wire to the open loop at the top of the earring.

6. Repeat all steps to make a second earring.

Blossoms

These flower hair pins will take care of any bad hair day. Make a trio with beads in complementary colors, and you'll hear nothing but compliments.

Finished size: 2½ inches (6.4 cm)

Materials (for a set of three)

3 antiqued brass dapped six-point filigree flowers, 20 mm

3 antiqued brass flat six-point filigree flowers, 20 mm

3 faceted or smooth round glass beads, 6 to 8 mm

18 faceted or smooth round glass beads, 4 mm

12 antiqued brass oval jump rings, 4 x 5 mm

3 brown bobby pins

Medium-width flexible beading wire, 3 feet (0.9 m)

Clear jeweler's adhesive cement (optional)

Tools

Wire cutters

Chain-nose pliers

Techniques

Knotting (page 27)

Sewing beads to filigree (page 26)

Opening and closing rings (page 25)

Instructions

1. Cut a 12-inch (30.5 cm) length of wire and string on an 8-mm bead, leaving a 4-inch (10.2 cm) tail. Sew the bead to the center of one of the dapped flowers. Tie a square knot on the back of the flower to firmly seat the bead (figure 1). Don't trim the wire.

fig. 1

2. Pass the long wire end to the front of the flower, exiting from a petal. String on one 4-mm bead and sew it to the petal (figure 2). Repeat around to add six 4-mm beads in all. Tie a square knot on the back of the flower and trim the excess wire. Set the beaded flower aside.

fig. 2

3. Slide one flat flower into a bobby pin so the pin hooks in the dip between petals. Place a beaded flower on top of the flat flower so the petals line up. Use jump rings to attach the top two and bottom two petal points (figure 3). ***Note:*** Though the flower may move slightly on the bobby pin, it should be secure. To reduce the movement, place a small drop of adhesive cement on the center back of the beaded flower before attaching it to the flat one.

fig. 3

4. Repeat all steps to make two more hair pins.

Elizabeth

A beaded filigree rosette, suspended from a strand of pearls, makes for a magnificent pendant. The elaborate bail is actually a flat piece of filigree, bent to shape.

Instructions

1. Cut a 36-inch (0.9 m) length of flexible wire, string on the smoke crystal bead, and slide it to the center. Pass the wire ends down through the center of the dapped rosette. Tie a square knot, but don't trim the wire.

2. Pass one wire end up through the filigree to exit next to one of the bead holes. String on two 4-mm pearl beads and pass down through the filigree so the pearl beads lay next to each other. Pass up through the filigree to exit next to the opposite bead hole and sew on two 4-mm pearl beads as before.

   Repeat to sew a pair of pearls to each side of the smoke crystal bead. The pearl pairs should be evenly spaced and firmly attached. **Note:** When beading this pendant, you need to keep substantial tension on the wire so the beads line up correctly. You may tie square knots as you work to keep the tension if you're having trouble holding it tight with your fingers.

3. Pass the long end of the wire up through the filigree to exit next to a pearl pair. String on one olive bicone bead and pass down through the filigree to seat the bead. Pass the wire across the back of the filigree where you just placed the bead, then pass it up through the filigree to exit from a hole just up from the crystal bead. This is row 2. Repeat, adding beads in stacked rows in this order: row 3, two pearl beads; row 4, one bicone bead, one pearl bead, and one bicone bead; row 5, two pearls beads (figure 1). At the end of the petal, tie a square knot to secure the beads.

fig. 1

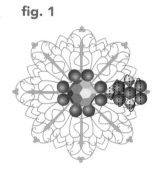

   Repeat to add beaded "petals" to the filigree in an *X* shape. If the working strand becomes too short, knot it and continue beading with the remaining wire strand. Pass one end of the beading wire up through the filigree to exit next to an un-adorned pearl bead pair. String on one 8-mm pearl bead and sew it to the filigree.

Finished size: 30 inches (76.2 cm)

Materials

1 gold-plated dapped filigree floral rosette, 47 mm

1 gold-plated flat filigree floral rosette, 47 mm

1 gold-plated filigree connector bar, 10 x 30 mm

4 gold-plated dapped filigree wings, 25 x 30 mm

1 smoke metallic AB crystal round bead, 8 mm

104 olive crystal pearl round beads, 8 mm

32 olive AB crystal bicone beads, 4 mm

28 olive crystal pearl round beads, 4 mm

2 gold-filled round jump rings, 7 mm

2 gold-filled oval jump rings, 4 x 5 mm

4 gold-plated knot covers, 4 mm

9 x 11-mm gold-plated double curb chain, 15 inches (38.1 cm)

Gold-filled 20-gauge wire, 3 inches (7.6 cm)

Fine-width gold-colored flexible beading wire, 60 inches (1.5 m)

Green knotting silk, size 6

Tools and Techniques are listed on the following page.

Elizabeth

Tools

Round-nose pliers

Chain-nose pliers

Wire cutters

Techniques

Knotting (page 27)

Simple loop (page 22)

Opening and closing rings (page 25)

Bending filigree (page 28)

Sewing beads to filigree (page 26)

fig. 2   **fig. 3**

fig. 4

4. Pass the wire across the back of the filigree and up through to exit from a hole just above the pearl (figure 2). String on two olive bicone beads and sew the beads just above the 8-mm pearl bead.

Repeat to add three more petals to the filigree in an *X* shape. Knot all remaining wire lengths and trim. Set the beaded rosette aside.

5. Use chain-nose pliers to grasp the connector bar at its midpoint and make a 45° bend. Make two more bends on each side of the initial bead to create a *U* shape. Maintaining the *U* shape, gently press the bar's ends together.

6. Open a round jump ring and attach it to one of the end holes on the bar. Stack the rosettes back to back and slide them onto the jump ring at a petal point. Close the ring. Repeat with the remaining round jump ring, connecting to the next petal point.

7. Use oval jump rings to connect the two pairs of petals at the bottom of the rosette (figure 3). Set the pendant aside.

8. Tie a surgeon's knot at the end of the knotting silk and string on a knot cover from inside to outside (figure 4). String on forty-seven 8-mm pearl beads and a knot cover from outside to inside. Knot the silk close to the knot cover and trim. Use chain-nose pliers to gently close the knot covers. Set aside.

Repeat with the remaining silk, knot covers, and fifty-three 8-mm pearl beads to create a second strand.

9. Cut a 1-inch (2.5 cm) length of gold-filled wire. Form a simple loop at one end. Slide on one olive bicone bead and form a simple loop to secure it. Repeat to create six bead links in all. Set aside.

10. Cut a 12-inch (30.5 cm) length of beading wire and use it to sew three olive bicone beads to the center of one of the filigree wings. Stack the beaded and non-beaded sets of wings back to back. Use one beaded link to connect the top of the wings and one beaded link each to connect the bottom of the wings (figure 5). Repeat with the remaining filigree wings. Set aside.

11. Attach one end of the chain to the open loop at the top of one set of wings. Repeat for the other end of the chain and the remaining set of wings.

12. Pass the 53-bead strand through the bail at the top of the pendant.

13. Lay the pendant and wings face-side-up. Connect the knot cover at one end of the pearl strand to the right outside wing (figure 6). Connect the knot cover on the opposite end of the strand to the left outside wing. Connect the knot cover on one end of the 47-bead strand to the right inside wing. Connect the cover at the opposite end of the strand to the inside left wing.

fig. 5

fig. 6

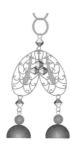

Joie de Vivre

Slip this ring on your finger and suddenly a waiter will be at your elbow, refilling your drink before you ask. A suave man will inquire if he didn't, perhaps, see you last week in Cannes? Fabulous at a party, this ring mixes crystals and pearls and will add excitement even to trips to the grocery.

Finished size: 5 cm ring top

Materials

1 silver-plated dapped filigree cross, 50 mm

12 smoke metallic AB round crystal beads, 3 mm

6 black crystal pearl round beads, 4 mm

1 teal channel-backed rhinestone, 6 mm

1 silver-plated round screen ring finding (ring base only), 26 mm ring top

Silver medium-width flexible beading wire, 30 inches (76.2 cm)

Tools

Wire cutters

Chain-nose pliers

Techniques

Sewing beads to filigree (page 26)

Knotting (page 27)

Instructions

1. Cut the wire into two 12-inch (30.5 cm) lengths and one 6-inch (15.2 cm) length. Set aside.

2. Pass the short wire length through the back of the rhinestone. Sew the rhinestone to the front center of the filigree cross. Tie a square knot on the back of the cross to firmly seat the rhinestone. Trim the wire ends and set aside.

3. Use a long wire to string on eight 3-mm beads, leaving a 3-inch (7.6 cm) tail. Tie a square knot to make a tight circle. Don't trim the wire ends. Set aside.

4. Use the third wire to string on the remaining 3-mm and 4-mm beads in an alternating pattern, leaving a 3-inch (7.6 cm) tail, as shown in figure 1. Tie a square knot to make a tight circle. Don't trim the wire ends. Set aside.

fig. 1

5. Place the 3-mm bead circle around the rhinestone. Pass the wire ends down through the filigree next to the circle. Pass the long wire end up through the filigree between the circle's next two beads. Cross the wire between the beads and pass down through the filigree to seat the circle (figure 2). Pass up through the filigree, exiting between the circle's next two beads, cross the wire between the beads, and pass down through the filigree as before. Continue around to sew the circle firmly to the filigree. Knot the wire ends and trim.

fig. 2

6. Repeat step 5, adding the 3- and 4-mm bead circle around the circle just placed.

7. Center the back of the filigree on the face of the ring base. Note the place where the prongs on the form fit into the filigree. Use chain-nose pliers to grasp a prong and carefully bend it over the filigree. Repeat with each prong to attach the filigree to the ring base. Work from side to side, not clockwise, to make sure the filigree remains centered.

Louise

Flirty and a bit bohemian, these earrings take advantage of the visual weight of filigree. While they look almost too heavy for your ears, they feel just like feathers.

Materials

2 antiqued brass six-point dapped filigree flowers, 20 mm

2 antiqued brass six-point flat filigree flowers, 20 mm

2 antiqued brass filigree rings, 32 mm

2 peach crystal round beads, 6 mm

2 amber flat diamond glass beads with gold-colored design, 7 x 12 mm

2 antiqued brass head pins, 2 inches (5.1 cm)

6 antiqued brass oval jump rings, 4 x 5 mm

1 pair of antiqued brass ear wires

Medium-width flexible beading wire, 12 inches (30.5 cm)

Tools

Chain-nose pliers

Round-nose pliers

Wire cutters

Techniques

Opening and closing rings (page 25)

Wrapped loops (page 24)

Sewing beads to filigree (page 26)

Instructions

1. Pass a head pin through the edge of a filigree ring from inside to outside (figure 1). Slip on one round bead and form a wrapped loop to secure the bead. Set aside.

2. Cut a 6-inch (15.2 cm) length of wire and string on a diamond bead, leaving a 3-inch (7.6 cm) tail. Sew the bead to the center of one of the dapped flowers. Tie a square knot on the back of the flower to firmly seat the bead. Trim the wire ends.

3. Place the dapped flower on top of one of the flat flowers so their backs touch. Use a jump ring to connect each of the petal sets.

4. Attach one of the jump rings on the flower to the wrapped loop formed in step 1 (figure 2). This is the bottom of the earring.

5. Use a jump ring to attach the ear wire to the jump ring at the top of the earring.

6. Repeat all steps to make a second earring.

fig. 1   **fig. 2**

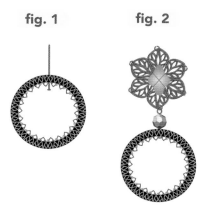

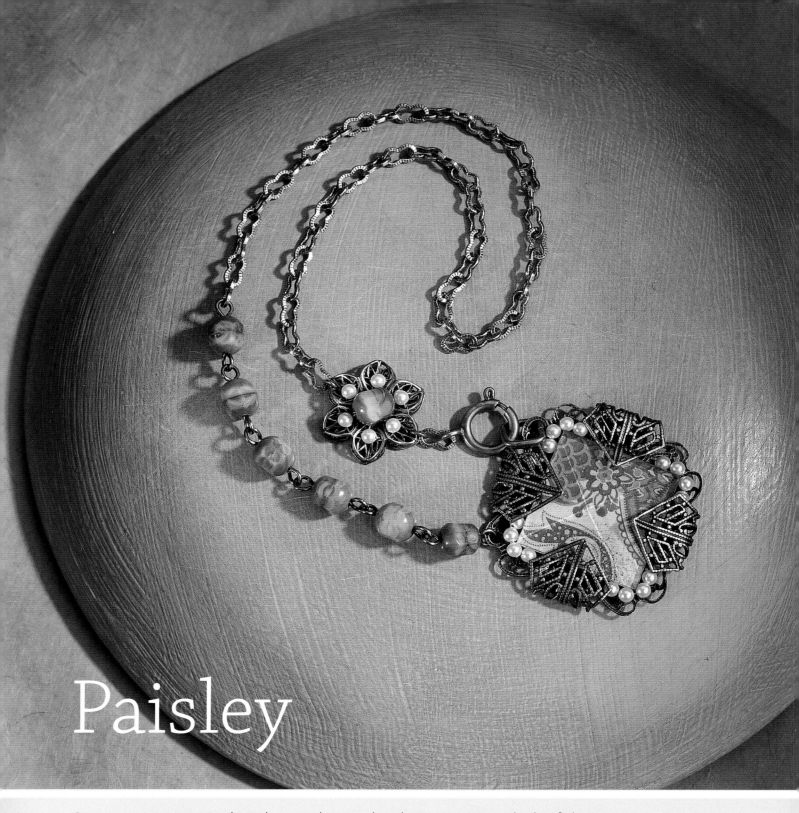

Paisley

Going asymmetrical makes a design both exciting and playful. Because it's unexpected, putting the clasp front and center adds an interesting touch, and inserting pretty wrapping paper beneath the glass keeps the piece unique.

Instructions

1. Lay the paper on the work surface and place the glass square on top. Trace around the outside of the glass and trim the paper on the line. Take care to make the cut just inside the tracing's perimeter so it doesn't overhang.

2. Place a pea-size drop of adhesive on the back of the glass. Use your finger or the sponge-tip paintbrush to spread the adhesive over the entire surface. Place the paper, pattern side down, on the glass and smooth it with your finger until the paper is very smooth.

3. Place a half-pea-size drop of adhesive on the back of the paper and smooth it with your finger (figure 1). Set the glass aside to dry, face down.

fig. 1

4. Cut a 12-inch (30.5 cm) length of flexible wire and string on a barrel bead, leaving a 4-inch (10.2 cm) tail. Sew the bead to the center of one of the dapped flowers. Tie a square knot on the back of the flower to firmly seat the bead. Pass the long wire end to the front of the flower, exiting from a petal. String on one pearl bead and sew it to the petal. Repeat around to add six pearl beads in all. Tie a square knot on the back of the flower and trim the excess wire. Set the beaded flower aside.

5. Stack the beaded flower and the flat flower back to back, petals aligned. Use a jump ring to connect one pair of petals. Use another jump ring to connect the opposite pair of petals (figure 2). Set aside.

fig. 2

Note

A photo, piece of sheet music, or other type of paper can be substituted for the wrapping paper. A square cabochon could also be used instead of paper and glass.

Finished size: 17 inches (43.2 cm)

Materials

1 antiqued brass dapped filigree cross, 50 mm square

1 antiqued brass six-pointed dapped flower filigree, 20 mm

1 antiqued brass six-pointed flat flower filigree, 20 mm

7 purple, blue, green, and brown givré glass barrels, 6 x 8 mm

22 white crystal pearls, 3 mm

2 antiqued brass jump rings, 3 x 4 mm

1 square brass jump ring, ¼ inch (6 mm)

1 antiqued brass spring ring clasp, 14 mm

7 x 4-mm link antiqued brass peanut chain, 11 inches (27.9 cm)

Antiqued brass 20-gauge wire, 7½ inches (19.1 cm)

Medium-width flexible beading wire, 28 inches (71.1 cm)

1 clear glass bevel, 1 x 1 inch (2.5 x 2.5 cm)

Purple, yellow, and blue paisley wrapping paper or scrapbook paper, at least 1 x 1 inch (2.5 x 2.5 cm)

Water-based dimensional adhesive glaze

Tools and Techniques are listed on the following page.

Tools

Pencil

Scissors or razor knife

Sponge-tip paintbrush

Chain-nose pliers

Round-nose pliers

Wire cutters

Techniques

Sewing beads to filigree (page 26)

Knotting (page 27)

Opening and closing rings (page 25)

Simple loop (page 22)

Metal forming (page 28)

6. Cut a 1¼-inch (3.2 cm) length of brass wire. Form a simple loop at one end. Slide on one barrel bead and form a simple loop to secure it. Repeat to make six bead links. Connect the links together, end to end, to make a beaded chain. Set aside.

7. Remove an end link of the peanut chain and set it aside. Open the next link on the chain and attach it to an end loop of the beaded chain. Connect the other end of the peanut chain to one of the jump rings on the beaded flower. Use the single chain link to connect the flower's remaining jump ring and the clasp (figure 3). Set aside.

fig. 3

8. Lay the cross facedown on the work surface. Place the glass, faceup, in the center of the cross. Decide where you'd like the points of the cross to bend up and over the glass. It may be useful to sketch the shape of the filigree and note the bend points on the sketch while working.

9. Remove the glass from the cross. Use chain-nose pliers to gently bend the points of the filigree up to form right angles. Place the glass back into the center of the cross.

10. Working from side to side, use chain-nose pliers to slowly and carefully bend each point over the glass. Take care to not scratch the glass surface with the pliers. *Note:* If the glass is loose, use chain-nose pliers to carefully tighten the fit, continuing to work from side to side, not clockwise. To create an even setting, make many small adjustments rather than a few large ones. Set the pendant aside.

11. Cut a 4-inch (10.2 cm) length of flexible wire and string on four pearl beads. Slide them to the center. Working from the front of the filigree on one corner of the pendant, pass both ends of the wire through the filigree holes. Tie a square knot to secure the beads (figure 4). Trim the excess wire. Repeat to add pearl beads to all four corners.

fig. 4

12. Open the end link of the beaded chain and attach it to the upper left corner of the pendant. Attach the square jump ring to the upper right corner of the pendant.

Queen Anne's Lace

This simple necklace features a whitewashed filigree rosette beaded with glass pearls. The mix of whitewashed metal and brass makes the design casual. The double chain allows you to wear it long or short.

Instructions

1. Cut the chain into two 18-inch sections with one oval link at each end. Set aside.

2. Heat-treat the rosettes and clean them so they're free of lint or dust. Set aside.

3. Working in a well-ventilated area, set a few sheets of newsprint or scrap cardboard down to protect your work surface. Spray the front of both rosettes with a thin coat of clear paint. Immediately spray a thin coat of white over the clear paint and use a cloth to rub the paint from the surface. Some paint will remain in the details of the filigree. To add or reduce the amount of paint in the finish, spray the rosettes with white paint again. Immediately wipe the paint. Once you are pleased with the effect, allow the paint to dry for two hours. After it has dried, apply two thin coats of clear paint, allowing the paint to dry thoroughly between coats. Set aside.

4. Repeat step 3 with the chain sections. Take care to thoroughly wipe the chain from end to end.

5. Slide one 8-mm bead and the bead cap, inside to outside, onto a head pin. Form a simple loop to secure the bead and cap. Set this long dangle aside.

6. Slip one 3-mm bead onto a head pin. Form a simple loop to secure the bead. Repeat to make small dangles with all the 3-mm beads. Set aside.

7. Attach one small dangle to each of the center oval links that sit between the chain's long tube sections (figure 1). There should be one remaining link. Set aside.

fig. 1

Finished size: 36 inches (.9 m)

Materials

2 brass filigree rosettes, 30 mm

59 white glass pearl round beads, 3 mm

1 white glass pearl round bead, 8 mm

1 antiqued brass petal bead cap, 6 mm

43 antiqued brass 22-gauge head pins, 1 inch (2.5 cm)

1 antiqued brass 20-gauge head pin, 1 inch (2.5 cm)

1 antiqued brass square jump ring, ¼ inch (6 mm)

3 antiqued brass round jump rings, 7 mm

1 antiqued brass spring ring clasp, 15 mm

2 x 15-mm link antiqued brass filled tube chain, 36 inches (91.4 cm)

Medium-width flexible beading wire, 12 inches (30.8 cm)

Clear enamel spray paint

White enamel spray paint

Newsprint or scrap cardboard

Soft cloth

Tools and Techniques are listed on the following page.

Tools

Wire cutters

Round-nose pliers

Chain-nose pliers

Techniques

8. Place the rosettes back to back, edges aligned. Pass the beading wire through a hole at the edge of the two pieces and tie a square knot, leaving a 4-inch (10.2 cm) tail, as shown in figure 2.

String on one 3-mm bead and sew around the edge of the rosettes, passing through the next hole (figure 3). Repeat around to add sixteen 3-mm beads in all. Tie a square knot with the working and tail wires and trim close to the knot. Set the pendant aside.

9. Open a round jump ring and attach it to a hole at the edge of the pendant. Slip on the long dangle and close the ring. Attach a round jump ring to a hole on the opposite edge of the ring just placed (figure 4).

10. Use the square jump ring to connect one end of each chain length and the top of the pendant (figure 5).

11. Use chain-nose pliers to gently open the loop on the spring ring clasp. Attach the open ends of the chain and close the loop.

12. Open a round jump ring and slide on the remaining small dangle and the clasp loop. Close the ring (figure 6). To wear the necklace short, connect the clasp to the square jump ring. To wear it long, simply separate the chains and slip the necklace over your head.

fig. 2

fig. 3

fig. 4

fig. 5

fig. 6

Coral Fringe

With a mix of metals and colors, this brooch is fun and feminine. Try pinning it in an unexpected place, like the waist of a dress or the hip pocket of a corduroy jacket.

Coral Fringe

Materials

1 silver dapped eight-point flower filigree, 47 mm

1 natural brass flat vines filigree, 30 x 55 mm

1 green jasper round cabochon, approximately 32 mm

18 orange coral beads, 5 to 7 mm

6 antiqued brass square jump rings, ½ inch (6 mm)

6 antiqued brass head pins, 1 inch (2.5 cm)

18 silver head pins, 1 inch (2.5 cm)

1 silver brooch set (backing only), ¾ inch (1.9 cm)

Fine-width flexible beading wire, 20 inches (50.8 cm)

Clear industrial-strength craft adhesive

Tools

Wire cutters

Chain-nose pliers

Wire cutters

Wooden spoon

Techniques

Opening and closing rings (page 25)

Simple loop (page 22)

Knotting (page 27)

Forming filigree (page 28)

Bending metal (page 29)

Instructions

1. Cut the wire into two 10-inch (25.4 cm) pieces. Set aside.

2. Set the stone in the center of the flower filigree and consider how the curved metal will wrap around it. Decide where on the filigree the bends should occur to neatly wrap the stone. It may be useful to sketch the shape of the filigree and mark the bend points on the sketch. Keep in mind that the stone's back should sit on the filigree so that when the metal is bent around it, the curved front will show.

3. Following the sketch, use chain-nose pliers to grasp one petal and bend it up into a 90° angle. Repeat to bend all the petals (figure 1). Work with the filigree slowly and carefully, stopping frequently to slide the stone into place and check the fit. Move from petal to petal, bending each side carefully, frequently stopping to test the fit of your stone.

   fig. 1

   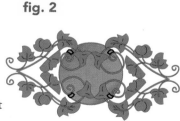

4. Fit the top two tabs of the pin back into the vines filigree as shown (figure 2). The pin back should sit slightly above center. Remove the pin back and apply a drop of glue to the metal. Immediately reposition it against the filigree and use chain-nose pliers to squeeze the prongs into place. Let the glue dry completely.

   fig. 2

   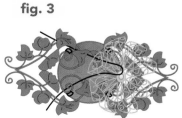

5. Place the back of the filigree flower on top of the flat vines filigree. Pass one piece of wire from the back to the front of the pin, over the filigree flower along the side of the pin back, and back down through the vines filigree. Tie a knot (figure 3). Repeat on the other side of the pin back to firmly seat the filigree. Trim the wire ends.

   fig. 3

   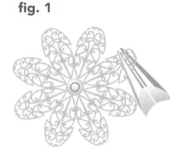

6. Slide one brass head pin through one of the bottom loops of the filigree flower. Trim the head pin to ½ inch (1.3 cm) and form a simple loop. Repeat with the remaining brass head pins to create six separate loops along the bottom of the pin (figure 4).

fig. 4

7. Slip one coral bead on one silver head pin and form a simple loop to secure the bead. Set aside. Repeat to make 18 dangles in all.

8. Open a square jump ring, attach three dangles, and connect the ring to one of the loops at the bottom of the pin. Repeat so that each loop at the bottom of the pin has an embellished jump ring attached.

9. Place the stone onto the flower filigree. Use chain-nose pliers to push the petals closer to the stone. Work slowly—lots of tightening a little bit at a time will result in a more even stone setting. Work from side to side, not clockwise, to keep the stone centered. Finally, use a wooden spoon to press the tips of the filigree petals toward the stone.

Violet

These classic earrings are the perfect accompaniment to a proper suit. Beaded with a mix of purples, this technique allows you to completely cover a filigree shape with sparkle and shine.

Finished size: 1½ inches (3.8 cm)

Materials

2 silver-plated dapped five-point filigree flowers, 35 mm

2 silver-plated flat five-point filigree flowers, 35 mm

40 dark purple crystal pearl beads, 4 mm

30 amethyst crystal bicone beads, 4 mm

20 purple crystal bicone beads, 4 mm

2 silver-plated flat-face earring posts, 20 mm

Medium-width silver-tone flexible beading wire, 4 yards (3.7 m)

E-6000 glue

Tools

Wire cutters

Round-nose pliers

Chain-nose pliers

Techniques

Knotting (page 27)

Sewing beads to filigree (page 26)

Opening and closing rings (page 25)

Simple loop (page 22)

Instructions

1. Cut a 6-inch (15.2 cm) length of wire. String on five pearl beads and use the wire ends to tie a tight square knot, creating a bead circle. Use the ends to sew the circle to the center of one of the dapped filigree forms.

2. Cut a 12-inch (30.5 cm) length of wire. Pass both ends through the filigree at the base of the petal, from front to back, leaving a 4-inch (10.2 cm) tail, as shown in figure 1. Tie a square knot to secure the wire. Don't trim.

fig. 1

3. Pass the long end of the wire up through the filigree at the petal's base. String on one amethyst and one purple crystal bead. Cross the strand across the width of the petal and pass down through the filigree. Pass the wire across the back of the petal and up through a filigree hole just up from the first bead placed in the first row (figure 2). Repeat, adding rows of beads across the front of the petal in this order: row 2, two pearl beads; row 3, one amethyst, one purple, and one amethyst crystal bead; row 4, one pearl bead. Tie the wire ends together in a tight square knot and trim.

fig. 2

4. Repeat steps 2 and 3 for the remaining petals.

fig. 3

5. Stack the beaded flower and a flat flower with backs touching. Cut a 12-inch (30.5 cm) length of wire. Use a square knot to attach the wire to the edge of one of the flat flowers, near a petal base. Leave a 4-inch (10.2 cm) tail.

6. Use the long wire to sew the edges of the top and bottom flowers together. Maintain a tight tension and be careful that the flowers don't shift while you're sewing them. When you reach the starting point, tie the wire ends in a square knot and trim (figure 3).

7. Place a small dot of glue on the flat face of one earring post. Press the post into the flat filigree at a point slightly above the center. Let dry for 24 hours before wearing.

8. Repeat all steps to make a second earring.

Carla

Ignore your to-do list as you wear this necklace, sipping coffee for hours with a friend. The striking design features an unusual color combination and the pretty toggle is placed near the front to show it off.

Materials

Finished size: 16 inches (40.6 cm)

1 antiqued brass dapped square filigree cross, 50 mm

1 antiqued brass filigree ring, 32 mm

1 antiqued brass filigree spacer bar, 10 x 30 mm

1 rust, green, blue, and pink flat round cloisonné bead, 42 mm

8 purple vintage swirled diamond glass beads, 15 mm

7 rust knot vintage glass beads, 12 mm

1 rust size 6° seed bead

1 antiqued brass 20-gauge head pin, 1 inch (2.5 cm)

2 antiqued brass oval jump rings, 4 x 5 mm

6 antiqued brass square jump rings, 9 mm

5 x 6-mm link antiqued brass chain, 15 inches (38.1 cm)

Gunmetal 20-gauge craft wire, 24 inches (61 cm)

Tools

Wire cutters

Chain-nose pliers

Round-nose pliers

Techniques

Opening and closing rings (page 25)

Simple loops (page 22)

Forming filigree (page 28)

Bending metal (page 29)

Instructions

1. Cut the chain in one 14-inch (35.6 cm) length. Set this and the remaining 1-inch (2.5 cm) piece of chain aside.

2. Set the cloisonné bead on the back of the cross filigree, right in the center. Decide where the points of the cross will bend up and over the bead. It may be useful to sketch the pattern of the filigree and note the bend points on the sketch while working.

3. Use your fingers to gently bend the points of the filigree up to form right angles. Set the bead inside the filigree and continue to bend each point over the bead (figure 1).

fig. 1

Use chain-nose pliers to flatten the points down onto the bead. Take care not to scratch the bead's surface with the pliers. ***Note:*** If the bead is loose, use chain-nose pliers to carefully tighten the fit, working slowly from side point to side point—not clockwise. To create an even setting, make many small adjustments rather than a few large ones. Set the pendant aside.

4. Place the spacer bar on top of the filigree ring. Note the points where the bar overlaps the ring. Use chain-nose pliers to make a 45° bend at one of the points. Repeat to make a matching bend at the other end of the spacer bar (figure 2).

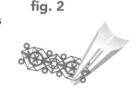

fig. 2

5. Slip the seed bead on the head pin. Pass the head pin through the spacer bar's center hole from front to back. Trim the head pin to ⅜ inch (9 mm) and form a simple loop to secure the bead (figure 3). Use a square jump ring to attach the loop on the back of the spacer bar to the end link of the 1-inch (2.5 cm) piece of chain. Set the toggle bar aside.

fig. 3

6. Cut a 1½-inch (3.8 cm) length of wire and form a simple loop at one end. Slide on one purple bead and form a simple loop to secure it. Repeat to create one-bead links with all the purple and rust beads.

fig. 4

fig. 5

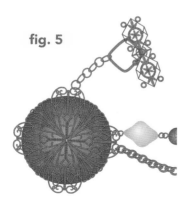

7. Attach the end of one purple bead link to the end of one rust bead link. Continue, connecting all the links to make an alternating-bead chain.

8. Connect an end loop of the bead chain to a side loop on the pendant. Use an oval jump ring to attach the end of the 14-inch piece of (35.6 cm) chain to the pendant's adjacent side loop (figure 4).

9. Use a square jump ring to connect the open ends of the bead-link chain and the 14-inch piece of (35.6 cm) chain and to the filigree ring.

10. Move clockwise around the back of the pendant from the chains already placed. Note the next loop and use an oval jump ring to connect the toggle-bar chain to that loop (figure 5).

11. Open a square jump ring and lay the bead-link chain inside it between the third and fourth links. Lay the adjacent metal chain inside, too. Close the ring. Repeat with the remaining square jump rings, placing one square jump ring between each group of three bead links. Take care to loop the jump ring around the bead-link and metal chains, not through the chains.

Lotus

This looks like something inherited from a glamorous fourth cousin who danced in the Paris ballet before the war, married well, and finished life hosting intimate dinner parties for notorious friends. Not related to this dazzling creature? Make her proud anyway and wear it daily.

Finished size: 6½ inches (16.5 cm)

Materials

7 antiqued brass dapped six-point filigree flowers, 20 mm

7 antiqued brass flat six-point filigree flowers, 20 mm

7 translucent white crystal round beads, 8 mm

24 light topaz AB crystal round beads, 4 mm

18 opaque pink crystal round beads, 4 mm

1 antiqued brass two-hole screen box clasp (clasp only), 20 mm

38 antiqued brass oval jump rings, 4 x 5 mm

Fine-width flexible beading wire, 3 yards (2.7 m)

Tools

Chain-nose pliers

Wire cutters

Techniques

Opening and closing rings (page 25)

Sewing beads to filigree (page 26)

Note

For a longer bracelet, add an additional flower link or use larger jump rings to connect the flowers.

Instructions

1. Cut a 12-inch (30.5 cm) length of wire and string on an 8-mm bead, leaving a 4-inch (10.2 cm) tail. Sew the bead to the center of one of the dapped flowers. Tie a square knot on the back of the flower to firmly seat the bead. Don't trim the wire.

2. Pass the long wire end to the front of the flower, exiting from a petal. String on one 4-mm pink bead and sew it to the petal. Repeat around to add six 4-mm pink beads in all. Tie a square knot on the back of the flower and trim the excess wire. Set the beaded flower aside.

3. Repeat steps 1 and 2 for all the dapped filigree flowers, creating three beaded flowers with pink 4-mm beads, and four with topaz 4-mm beads. Set all aside.

4. Place a beaded flower on top of a flat flower so their backs touch and the petals line up. Use a jump ring to attach the flat and dapped petals at four points: two petals at the left, and two at the right (figure 1). Set aside. Repeat to make three topaz and three pink two-sided flowers in all.

fig. 1

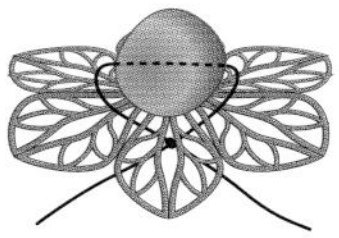

5. Remove the clasp's tongue and set it aside. Note the places where the prongs on the box half of the clasp could fit into the filigree of the remaining flat flower. Center the flat flower, front side down, onto the face of the box. Position the flower so one of its petals sits between the clasp loops. Use chain-nose pliers to grasp a prong and carefully bend it over the filigree (figure 2). Avoid scratching the clasp with the pliers. Repeat with each prong to attach the flat flower to the clasp. Work from side to side, not clockwise, to make sure the flower remains centered.

fig. 2

fig. 3

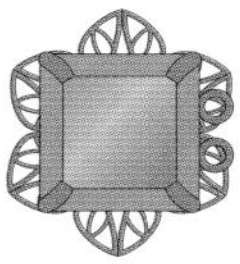

6. Place the remaining topaz beaded flower on top of the flower attached to the box clasp, lining up the petals. Use one jump ring to connect each pair of petals (figure 3).

7. Line up the remaining beaded flowers, alternating colors. Orient the flowers so the petal pairs without jump rings point up and down and the jump-ringed petal pairs sit at left and right. Use a jump ring to attach the adjacent pairs of rings to make a chain. Use jump rings to attach one end of the chain to the loops on the box half of the clasp; use two jump rings on each side to attach the tab half of the clasp (figure 4).

fig. 4

Florentine Lace

Have you received an invite to a masquerade ball held in an Italian Renaissance *palazzo*? These delicate earrings would be just the thing to flaunt. Or if you prefer, make a single square to dangle as a pendant from a velvet ribbon.

Materials

18 antiqued brass square filigree pieces, 15 mm

6 green round crystal beads, 4 mm

6 pink crystal round beads, 4 mm

6 blue crystal round beads, 4 mm

52 antiqued brass oval jump rings, 3 x 4 mm

1 pair of antiqued brass ear wires

Medium-width flexible beading wire, 36 inches (91.4 cm)

Tools

Chain-nose pliers

Round-nose pliers

Wire cutters

Techniques

Opening and closing rings (page 25)

Sewing beads to filigree (page 26)

Knotting (page 27)

Instructions

1. Lay out nine filigree squares in three rows of three to make one larger square.

2. Following the positions marked in figure 1, use jump rings to connect the squares. Check that the front of each filigree piece faces forward.

3. Cut one 2-inch (5.1 cm) length of wire and string on one green crystal bead. Starting with a corner filigree square, and working from the front center of that square, push both wire ends through the filigree holes. Tie a secure square knot. Trim the wire ends close to the knot. Repeat with all the filigree squares, following figure 2 for bead color placement. Take care to pass the wires through each square at the same angle so all the bead holes are parallel.

4. Connect a jump ring to the open hole of the corner green filigree square. Use another jump ring to attach the ring just placed to an ear wire (figure 2).

5. Repeat all steps to make a second earring.

fig. 1

fig. 2

Verdi

Elegant and delicate, this necklace features a two-step patina and subtle beading. Wear it to the symphony.

Finished size: 18 inches (45.7 cm)

Materials

2 natural brass filigree openwork rounded squares, 48 mm

1 natural brass filigree butterfly, 45 x 50 mm

4 jet crystal round beads, 8 mm

16 jet AB fire-polished round beads, 4 mm

1 gunmetal rhinestone ring, 25 mm

3 natural brass twisted oval rings, 10 mm

1 natural brass twisted fish hook clasp, 15 mm

4 x 5-mm natural brass hammered link chain, 20 inches (50.8 cm)

Thin-width bronze-colored flexible beading wire, 52 inches (1.3 m)

Newsprint or scrap cardboard

Dark green enamel spray paint

Light green enamel spray paint

Clear enamel spray paint

Soft cotton rag

Tools

Wire cutters

Chain-nose pliers

Techniques

Heat-treating (page 30)

Painting filigree (page 31)

Bending filigree (page 29)

Sewing beads to filigree (page 26)

Opening and closing rings (page 25)

Instructions

1. Cut the chain into two 10-inch (25.4-cm) pieces. Set aside.

2. Heat-treat one of the squares, the chain, and findings. Make sure they're free of lint or dust.

3. Working in a well-ventilated area, set a few sheets of newsprint or scrap cardboard down to protect your work surface. Spray the front of the square with a coat of dark green paint. Immediately wipe off the paint with the rag. Set aside to let dry. Repeat for both sides of the butterfly, the findings, and the chain.

4. Repeat step 3 with the light green spray paint. Let dry for at least two hours. Spray all the pieces with a thin coat of clear spray paint. Let dry for at least two hours.

5. Use chain-nose pliers to bend each butterfly wing 45° up from the sides of the body. Set aside.

6. Cut a 4-inch (10.2 cm) length of wire. Center the rhinestone ring on the painted square. Find a point where the ring and filigree touch and use the wire to tie the ring down with a square knot. Trim the wire ends. Repeat with a second 4-inch (10.2 cm) length of wire on the opposite side of the ring (figure 1).

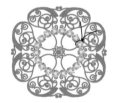

fig. 1

7. Cut a 12-inch (30.5 cm) length of wire and string on four crystal beads. Tie the beads into a tight circle using a square knot and leaving a 4-inch (10.2 cm) tail. Place the crystal circle inside the rhinestone loop. Pass the wire ends down through the filigree. Use the long wire end to sew the bead circle to the square (figure 2). Tie the wire ends with a square knot and trim.

fig. 2

8. Place the butterfly at an angle on one of the corners of the painted square. Cut a 12-inch (30.5 cm) length of wire and use it to sew the sides of the butterfly's body to the filigree. Use a square knot to tie the wire ends and trim.

9. Stack the squares back to back. Use the remaining wire to tie the squares' edges together with a square knot, leaving a 4-inch (10.2 cm) tail. String on a fire-polished bead and sew it to the edge of the squares, looping the wire around the edge and passing up through the filigree, making sure the bead stays toward the front of the painted square (figure 3). Repeat around the squares to sew on all the fire-polished beads, connecting the squares at the same time. Use a square knot to tie the wire ends and trim.

10. Use a decorative jump ring to connect the end of one chain to the filigree just to the left of the butterfly. Attach the clasp to the other end of the chain.

11. Use a decorative jump ring to connect the remaining chain to the filigree just to the right of the butterfly. Attach the remaining jump ring to the other end of the chain.

fig. 3

Camille

This choker-style necklace is strung on steel wire that holds its round shape, making it snug without being tight. Matching earrings complete the set. The dramatic dangles move as you walk, gesture, and dance.

Finished size: Adjustable, from 14 to 16 inches (35.6 to 40.6 cm)

Materials

Necklace

20 antiqued copper filigree bead caps, 8 mm

10 light purple fire-polished beads, 10 mm

12 light purple givré fire-polished beads, 8 mm

9 light purple fire-polished beads, 6 mm

16 light purple fire-polished beads, 4 mm

22 antiqued copper five-petal bead cones, 4 x 6 mm

6 antiqued copper chain links, 5 x 6 mm

4 antiqued copper head pins, 1 inch (2.5 cm)

1 antiqued copper fishhook clasp, 19 mm

Necklace-size memory wire, 12 inches (30.5 cm)

Gunmetal 20-gauge craft wire, 21 inches (53.3 cm)

Earrings

2 antiqued copper filigree bead caps, 8 mm

2 light purple fire-polished beads, 10 mm

2 mottled light purple fire-polished beads, 8 mm

4 antiqued copper five-petal bead cones, 4 x 6 mm

4 antiqued copper chain links, 5 x 6 mm

2 antiqued copper head pins, 1 inch (2.5 cm)

2 antiqued copper lever-back earring findings

Gunmetal 20-gauge craft wire, 4 inches (10.2 cm)

Instructions

Necklace

1. Cut a 1-inch (2.5 cm) length of wire. Form a simple loop at one end. Slide on one 6-mm bead and form a simple loop to secure it. Repeat to make nine bead links. Attach six links together, end to end, to make a long beaded chain, and two links together to make a short beaded chain. Set aside.

2. Slide one bead cap from outside to inside, one 10-mm bead, and one bead cap from inside to outside onto a head pin. Form a simple loop to secure the caps and bead. Repeat to make four drops in all. Set aside.

3. Cut a 2-inch (2.5 cm) length of wire. Form a simple loop at one end. Slip on one bead cap from outside to inside, one 10-mm bead, and one bead cap from inside to outside. Form a simple loop to secure the beads. Repeat for the remaining 10-mm beads to make six large bead links. Set aside.

fig. 1

4. Use chain-nose pliers to gently open one chain link. Use the link to connect one drop and one large bead link. Gently open another link and use it to connect the open end of the large bead link to a second large bead link (figure 1). Repeat two more times to make three long dangles in all. Set aside.

5. Form a simple loop at one end of the memory wire. Slide on a sequence of one 4-mm bead, one cone from outside to inside, one 6-mm bead, and one cone from inside to outside. Repeat the sequence four more times.

6. Slip on a sequence of one 4-mm bead, a long dangle, one 4-mm bead, and one 6-mm bead. Repeat the sequence once. Slide on one 4-mm bead, the open end of the remaining long dangle, and one 4-mm bead.

7. Repeat step 5 in reverse.

8. Attach the short chain to one end of the memory wire and the long chain to the other end. Attach the clasp to the open end of the short chain (figure 2).

   Connect the remaining drop to the open end of the long chain (figure 3).

Earrings

1. Cut the wire in two 2-inch (5.1 cm) pieces. Set aside.

2. Slide one 8-mm bead and one cone from inside to outside onto a head pin. Form a simple loop to secure the bead and cone. Set the drop aside.

3. Form a simple loop on one end of one wire. Slip on one bead cap from outside to inside, one 10-mm bead, and one bead cap from inside to outside. Form another simple loop to secure the caps and bead. Set the bead link aside.

4. Use chain-nose pliers to gently open one chain link. Use it to attach one drop to one bead link. Gently open a second link to attach the open end of the bead link to the earring finding.

5. Repeat steps 2 through 4 to make a second earring.

Tools
Wire cutters

Round-nose pliers

Chain-nose pliers

Techniques
Opening and closing rings (page 25)

Simple loop (page 22)

fig. 2   **fig. 3**

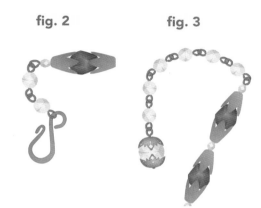

Eleanor

This elaborate necklace will make a stunning fashion statement with any ensemble. The design is easy to alter—just make one row of flowers for an understated look, or go all out with rows and rows of flowers.

Finished size: Adjustable, from 15 to 19 inches (38.1 to 48.3 cm)

Materials

22 antiqued brass dapped six-point filigree flowers, 20 mm

20 antiqued brass flat six-point filigree flowers, 20 mm

30 purple givré glass beads, 8 mm

52 opaque purple fire-polished beads, 4 mm

52 purple AB fire-polished beads, 4 mm

50 light purple fire-polished beads, 4 mm

160 antiqued brass oval jump rings, 4 x 5 mm

22 antiqued brass head pins, 1 inch (2.5 cm)

1 antiqued brass fishhook clasp, 19 mm

Fine-width flexible beading wire, 7 yards (6.4 m)

Antiqued brass 20-gauge wire, 38 inches (96.5)

Tools

Wire cutters

Round-nose pliers

Chain-nose pliers

Techniques

Simple loop (page 22)

Sewing beads to filigree (page 26)

Knotting (page 27)

Opening and closing rings (page 25)

Instructions

1. Cut a 1¼-inch (3.8 cm) length of brass wire and form a simple loop at one end. Slide on one 8-mm bead and form a simple loop to secure it. Repeat seven times to create eight bead links in all. Connect seven links together, end to end, to make a beaded chain. Set the chain and single bead link aside.

2. Select a mixed assortment of twenty-two 4-mm beads. Slide one onto a head pin and form a simple loop to secure the bead. Repeat to make 22 dangles in all. Set aside.

3. Cut a 12-inch (30.5 cm) length of beading wire and string on an 8-mm bead, leaving a 4-inch (10.2 cm) tail. Sew the bead to the center of one of the dapped flowers. Tie a square knot on the back of the flower to firmly seat the bead (figure 1). Don't trim the wire. Repeat for all the dapped flowers to create 22 beaded flowers in all.

fig. 1

4. Divide the remaining 4-mm beads by color. Pair each beaded flower with the six 4-mm beads that best complement the 8-mm beads.

5. Work with one beaded flower and the chosen beads. Pass the long wire end to the front of the flower, exiting from a petal. String on one 4-mm bead and sew it to the petal (figure 2). Repeat around to add six 4-mm beads in all. Tie a square knot on the back of the flower with the working and tail wires. Trim the excess wire. Set the beaded flower aside. Repeat for all the beaded flowers.

fig. 2

6. Select a beaded flower and line it up with a flat filigree flower, taking care that the front of the flat flower faces outward. Use jump rings to connect the tips of each pair of petals. Repeat for 20 beaded flowers in all. Set aside.

Place the remaining two beaded flowers back to back and connect their petal points in the same manner. Set aside.

7. Lay the beaded flowers in four rows: eleven in row 1, five in row 2, three in row 3, and one in row 4. Experiment with the placement of the individual flowers until you are pleased with how the bead shades and tones work together in the design.

8. Keeping the flowers in their rows, orient them so one petal points left, one right, two up, and two down. Use jump rings to connect the flowers of row 1 to each other at the side petal points. Repeat with rows 2 through 4.

fig. 3

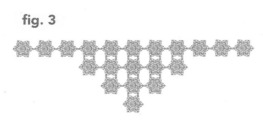

9. Use jump rings to connect rows 1 and 2. Start by connecting the bottom two jump rings of the fourth row 1 flower to the top two jump rings of the first row 2 flower. Continue across the row. In the same manner, connect the second row 2 flower to the first row 3 flower and finish connecting the two rows. Connect the row 4 flower to the middle row 3 flower (figure 3). While working, take care to keep the necklace as flat as possible.

fig. 4

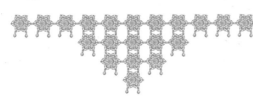

10. Attach a dangle to each bottom petal on the necklace that's not connected to another flower (figure 4).

11. Attach the bead chain to the petal at one end of row 1; connect the double-sided flower to the end of the chain. Attach the single bead link to the end petal at the other end of row 1; connect the clasp to the link.

Venice Jade

Imagine your great-grandmother wearing this bracelet with her favorite green dress. The layered filigree creates a substantial band and the central cabochon is set into a filigree wrap.

Finished size: Adjustable, from 7 to 8 inches (17.8 to 20.3 cm)

Materials

1 antiqued brass dapped filigree oval, 36 x 48 mm

14 antiqued brass filigree squares, 15 mm

1 semiprecious jade oval cabochon, approximately 22 x 35 mm

8 semiprecious jade flat round beads, 4 mm

32 antiqued brass 20-gauge oval jump rings, or sturdy chain links, 5 x 7 mm

1 antiqued brass oval jump ring, 4 x 5 mm

Medium-width flexible beading wire, 20 inches (50.8 cm)

Sketch paper (optional)

Tools

Pencil (optional)

Chain-nose pliers

Wire-cutters

Techniques

Forming filigree (page 28)

Sewing beads to filigree (page 26)

Opening and closing rings (page 25)

Instructions

fig. 1

1. Set the cabochon in the center of the oval so the back of the filigree and the back of the stone touch. The two pieces should be perpendicular (figure 1). Consider the best places to curve the filigree around the stone and note where the bends will occur. It may be useful to sketch the filigree's shape and mark the bend points.

2. Use chain-nose pliers to gently flatten the portion of the filigree that will lie underneath the cabochon. This will help create a tighter fit.

fig. 2

3. Following the marks noted earlier, use chain-nose pliers to wrap the filigree around the front of the cabochon (figure 2). Work slowly and carefully from side to side, stopping frequently to slide the cabochon into place to check the fit. Take care to avoid scratching the stone's surface with the pliers. *Note:* If the bead is loose, use chain-nose pliers to carefully tighten the fit, working slowly from side to side—not clockwise. To create an even setting, make many small adjustments rather than a few large ones. Set the focal piece aside.

4. String one 4-mm bead onto the beading wire, leaving a 4-inch (10.2 cm) tail. Push both wire ends through the holes on the front center of the filigree. Tie a tight square knot to secure the beads and trim. Repeat six times to embellish seven squares in all.

5. Place a beaded square on top of an unbeaded square, backs touching. Use the small jump ring to connect one pair of corners. Use a large jump ring to connect the corners at the diagonal. Set the square dangle aside.

6. Lay three unbeaded squares end to end on the work surface. The squares should be face down. Place one beaded square onto each of the unbeaded ones, face up. Use large jump rings to connect the squares at the adjacent corners. Add jump rings to connect the end corners as well (figure 3). Repeat to make a second three-square band.

fig. 3

7. Use one large jump ring to connect one corner at the end of one of the bands to the filigree on the focal piece. Repeat to attach the other corner (figure 4).

fig. 4

8. Repeat step 7 to connect the second band to the other side of the focal piece.

9. Link jump rings together to make three chains five jump rings long. Set aside.

fig. 5

10. Connect one end of a five-link chain to a jump ring on one end of the band. Connect the other end of the same chain to the jump ring on the other corner of the same band. Repeat at the other end of the band with the next five-link chain.

fig. 6

11. Open an end link on the remaining five-link chain and attach it to the center link of one of the chains placed in step. Close the link. Connect the other end of the chain to the large jump ring on the square dangle (figure 5).

12. Open the center link of the chain at the other end of the bracelet. Attach the link to the clasp (figure 6).

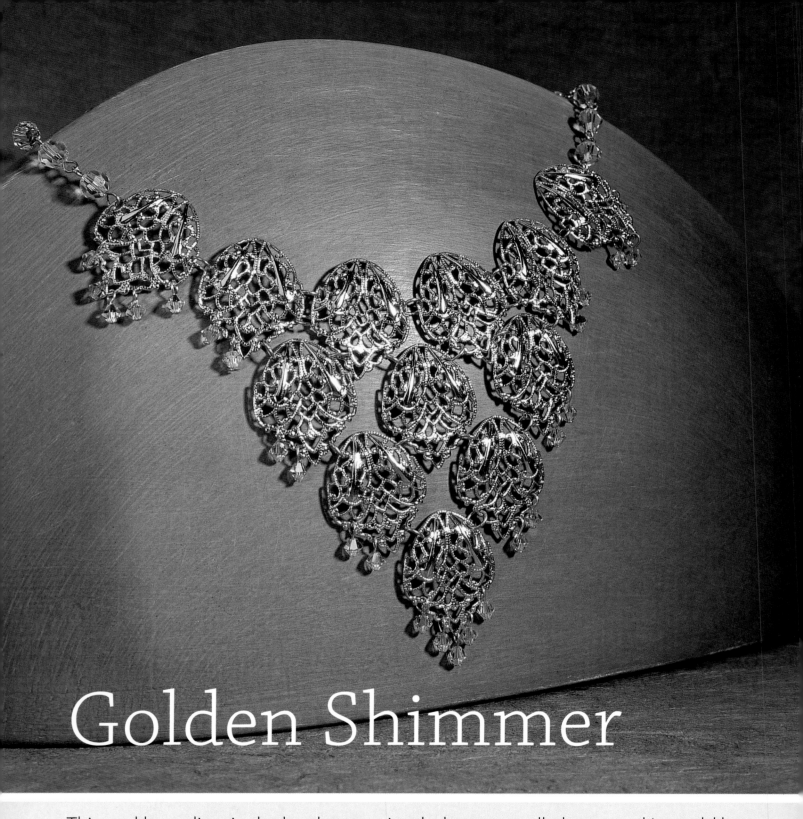

Golden Shimmer

This necklace glints in the lovely space just below your collarbone, and it would be perfect to wear to a summer cocktail party. The crystals along the bottom add a row of sparkle to this easy-to-make necklace and a beaded dangle in the back is an extra that will make heads turn.

Finished size: Adjustable, up to 18 inches (45.7 cm)

Materials

13 gold-filled filigree leaves, 12 mm x 26 mm

24 clear AB crystal round beads, 6 mm

28 clear AB crystal bicone beads, 4 mm

28 gold-filled head pins, 2 inches (5.1 cm)

20 gold-filled oval jump rings, 4 x 5 mm

1 gold-filled S clasp, 12 mm

Gold-filled 20-gauge wire, 36 inches (91.4 cm)

Tools

Chain-nose pliers

Round-nose pliers

Wire cutters

Techniques

Opening and closing rings (page 25)

Simple loop (page 22)

Instructions

1. Cut a 1-inch (2.5 cm) length of wire. Form a simple loop at one end. Slide on one 6-mm bead and form a simple loop to secure it. Repeat to make 24 bead links in all. Attach nine bead links together, end to end, to make one bead chain, and 15 links together to make a second chain. Set the short and long chains aside.

2. Slip a 4-mm bead onto a head pin. Form a simple loop to secure the bead. Repeat to create 28 dangles in all. Set aside.

3. Lay the filigree leaves in four rows: six leaves in row 1, three leaves in row 2, two leaves in row 3, and one leaf in row 4. Orient the leaves so their tips point down.

4. Make sure the leaves face forward as you connect the first leaf of row 1 to the second leaf using one jump ring. Attach the second leaf to the third using two jump rings. Connect the third to the fourth and the fourth to the fifth using two jump rings, and the fifth to the sixth using one jump ring.

5. Use a jump ring to connect the right bottom of the second leaf in row 1 to the left top of the first leaf in row 2. Use another jump ring to connect the right top of the first leaf in row 2 to the bottom left of the third leaf in row 1. Continue across, attaching the top of the row 2 leaves to the bottom of the row 1 leaves. In the same manner, attach row 3 to row 2 and row 4 to row 3 (figure 1).

fig. 1

fig. 2

6. Connect dangles to the holes at the bottom of the leaves, five to the first and last leaves in row 1; two dangles each to the holes at the bottom of the first and last leaves in rows 2 and 3; and five to the leaf in row 4 (figure 2). Periodically lift the necklace to your neck to see how the beads hang when the design is worn.

7. Attach five dangles to the remaining filigree leaf.

8. Connect the short chain to the left side of the first leaf in row 1 and the long chain to the right side of the last leaf in row 1. Attach the clasp to the end of the short chain and the remaining leaf to the end of the long chain. ***Note:*** If you'd rather not use the extender chain to fit the necklace, you may adjust for perfect fit by removing or adding bead links to the chains.

Helen

If Marie Antoinette were around, she'd beg you for this glamorous necklace. The mix of colors and beads makes it the perfect accompaniment for a simple formal dress as well as a fun piece to wear with more casual clothes.

Helen

Materials

1 antiqued brass dapped filigree square cross, 50 mm

1 antiqued brass filigree ring, 32 mm

2 antiqued brass dapped filigree rosettes, 28 mm

2 antiqued brass dapped filigree six-point flowers, 22 mm

2 antiqued brass flat filigree six-point flowers, 22 mm

1 antiqued brass dapped filigree eight-point oval, 36 x 48 mm

1 antiqued brass dapped five-point filigree flower, 20 mm

1 antiqued brass flat five-point filigree flower, 20 mm

1 blue dyed semiprecious jade oval cabochon, 18 x 36 mm

1 white opal crystal round bead, 8 mm

6 light pink crystal bicone beads, 6 mm

6 light blue opal crystal bicone beads, 6 mm

1 light red crystal round bead, 6 mm

11 aqua fire-polished glass round beads, 6 mm

9 acid green glass druk beads, 6 mm

31 fuchsia crystal round beads, 4 mm

8 acid green fire-polished glass round beads, 4 mm

16 turquoise blue fire-polished glass round beads, 4 mm

Instructions

1. Slide one green druk bead onto a head pin. Add one bead cap, inside to outside, and form a simple loop to secure the bead and cap. Repeat to create seven green bead dangles. Set aside.

   Repeat to create six aqua fire-polished bead dangles.

2. Cut a 1½-inch (3.8 cm) length of craft wire. Form a simple loop at one end. Slip on one bead cap from outside to inside, one green druk bead, and one bead cap from inside to outside. Form a simple loop to secure the caps and bead. Set the green bead link aside.

   Repeat once to make another green bead link. Repeat twice using 6-mm aqua beads.

3. Open a loop on a green bead link and attach it to one end of the chain. Close the loop. Attach the other end of the same bead link to an aqua bead link. Repeat for the other end of the chain. Set aside.

4. Cut a 12-inch (38.5 cm) length of beading wire. Place the rosettes back to back, edges aligned. Pass the beading wire through a hole at the edge of the two pieces and tie a square knot, leaving a 4-inch (10.2 cm) tail, as shown in figure 1.

   fig. 1

   String one 4-mm fuchsia bead onto the long end of the wire and sew around the edge of the paired rosettes, passing through the next hole as you go (figure 2). Make sure the beads stay on the side of the rosette and don't move to the front or back. Repeat around to add sixteen 4-mm beads in all. Tie a square knot with the working and tail wires and trim close to the knot.

   fig. 2

45 light red crystal round beads, 3 mm

21 antiqued brass petal bead caps, 4 x 6 mm

15 antiqued brass head pins, 1 inch (2.5 cm)

12 antiqued brass round jump rings, 5 mm

19 antiqued brass extra thick oval jump rings, 5 x 6 mm

1 antiqued brass square jump ring, 12 mm

5 x 6-mm link antiqued brass chain, 12 inches (38.5 cm)

Medium-width flexible beading wire, 6½ yards (5.9 m)

Gunmetal 20-gauge craft wire, 6 inches (15.2 cm)

Paper and pencil

Tools

Chain-nose pliers

Round-nose pliers

Wire cutters

Techniques

Opening and closing rings (page 25)

Simple loop (page 22)

Wrapped loop (page 24)

Knotting (page 27)

Sewing beads to filigree (page 26)

Bending filigree (page 29)

Attach the square jump ring to one side of the rosette and an oval jump ring to the opposite side. Set the beaded rosette aside.

5. Cut a 12-inch (30.5 cm) length of wire and string on a light red 6-mm round bead, leaving a 4-inch (10.2 cm) tail. Sew the bead to the center of a dapped six-point flower. Tie a square knot on the back of the flower to firmly seat the bead (figure 3).

fig. 3

Pass the long wire end to the front of the flower, exiting from a petal. String on one 6-mm blue opal bicone bead and sew it to the petal (figure 4). Repeat around to add six blue opal beads in all. Tie a square knot on the back of the flower and trim the excess wire.

fig. 4

Place the beaded flower on top of a flat six-point flower, backs touching and edges aligned. Use round jump rings to attach the flat and dapped petals at each of the six points (figure 5). Set aside.

fig. 5

Repeat this step to make another six-point beaded flower, this time using a 6-mm aqua bead for the center and 6-mm pink bicone beads for the petals.

6. Cut an 8-inch (20.3 cm) length of beading wire. String on the 8-mm white opal bead and slide it to the center of the wire. Pass the wire ends through the dapped oval so the bead is seated in the center. Pass the wire ends up through the filigree, knot securely, and trim the ends very close. ***Note:*** The knot is placed on the oval's front because the oval's back will be exposed in the finished design.

fig. 6

Cut a 12-inch (30.5 cm) length of beading wire and string on eight 4-mm green beads, leaving a 4-inch (10.2 cm) tail. Tie a square knot to make a tight circle of beads. Place the circle around the white opal bead and pass the wire ends down through the filigree. Pass the long wire end up through the filigree between the next two beads in the circle. Cross over the wire between beads and pass back down through the filigree (figure 6). Continue in this manner to completely sew the circle to the oval. Use the working and tail wires to tie a tight square knot and trim.

Attach one oval jump ring to one end of the filigree oval, and two evenly spaced oval jump rings to the opposite side. Set the filigree oval aside.

7. Lay the cross face down on the work surface. Place the cabochon, face up, in the center of the cross. Decide where you'd like the points of the cross to bend up and over the cabochon. It may be useful to sketch the shape of the filigree and note the bend points on the sketch while working. Remove the cabochon. Use chain-nose pliers to gently bend the points of the filigree up to form right angles. Place the cabochon back into the center of the cross. Working from side to side, use chain-nose pliers to slowly and carefully bend each point over the cabochon (figure 7). Take care to not scratch the stone's surface with the pliers. ***Note:*** If the cabochon is loose, use chain-nose pliers to carefully tighten the fit, continuing to work side to side, not clockwise. To create an even setting, make many small adjustments rather than a few large ones.

fig. 7

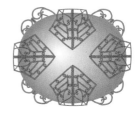

fig. 8

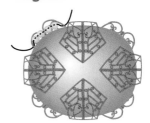

Cut a 4-inch (10.2 cm) length of beading wire and string on four 4-mm aqua beads. Slide them to the center. Working from the front of the filigree on one corner of the cabochon, pass both ends of the wire through the filigree holes (figure 8). Tie a square knot to secure the beads. Trim the excess wire. Repeat to add four beads to each corner.

Attach two evenly spaced oval jump rings to one end of the cross and a matching set on the opposite side. Set the jade oval aside.

8. Cut a 6-inch (15.2 cm) length of beading wire and string on five 4-mm fuchsia beads, leaving a 2-inch (5.1 cm) tail. Tie a square knot to make a tight bead circle. Center the circle on the dapped five-point flower and pass the wire ends down through the filigree. Pass the long wire up through the filigree and sew the circle down using the technique in figure 6. Knot the wire ends and trim.

Cut a 12-inch (30.5 cm) length of beading wire and pass it up through the filigree, exiting from the base of one of the petals and leaving a 4-inch (10.2 cm) tail. String on two 3-mm light red beads and pass down through the filigree so the beads sit side by side. Tie a square knot to secure the beads. This is row 1. Lay the wire across the back of the petal and pass up through the filigree, exiting just down the petal from the first bead strung. Repeat to make row 2, using one 3-mm light red bead, one 4-mm fuchsia bead, and one 3-mm light red bead (figure 9). Continue making rows in this order: row 3, two 3-mm light red beads; row 4, three 3-mm light red beads; and row 5, one 4-mm fuchsia bead. Tie a square knot with the wire ends and trim. Repeat for the remaining petals.

Stack the beaded flower and a flat five-point flower, backs touching. Cut a 12-inch (30.5 cm) length of wire. Use a square knot to attach the wire near the base of a petal on the flat flower, leaving a 4-inch (10.2 cm) tail. Use the long wire to sew the edges of the top and bottom flowers together. Maintain a tight tension. When you reach the starting point, tie the wire ends in a square knot (figure 10). Trim the wire ends.

Attach two oval jump rings to the end of one petal. Count two petals over and add one jump ring. Set the beaded five-point flower aside.

fig. 9

fig. 10

fig. 11

fig. 12

9. Pass a head pin through the edge of a filigree ring from inside to outside (figure 11).

   Slip on one 6-mm aqua bead and form a wrapped loop to secure the bead. Repeat for the opposite side of the ring (figure 12). Set the beaded ring aside.

10. Lay out the necklace elements in the order they were created, from steps 4 through 9. Make sure the pieces are all face up. Use one oval jump ring to connect each of the elements to the oval jump rings already placed on the pieces. **Note:** You'll need to connect the beaded ring by attaching oval jump rings to the wrapped loops.

11. Connect a bead link at the end of the chain to the square jump ring on the rosette. Attach the bead link at the other end of the chain to the round jump ring opposite the oval jump ring placed on the blue six-point flower.

12. Attach the bead dangles to the necklace in this order: two green dangles to the bottom two points of the pink six-point flower; three aqua dangles to the bottom of the filigree oval, making sure they're evenly spaced; one aqua and one green dangle to the bottom left of the cabochon oval, and one green and one aqua dangle to the bottom right; two green dangles to the petal nearest the cabochon oval; and one aqua and one green dangle to the bottom two points of the blue six-point flower.

Acknowledgments

This book has been a labor of love and I want to thank all those who helped me make it a reality.

My husband was endlessly patient and supportive, bringing me cup after cup of tea as I worked at my studio table late into the night, and setting his own projects aside to see this through. He has always supported my beading obsession and I can't thank him enough. My daughters, too, have been sweet and a breath of air when I needed to look up from the beads or the keyboard. They were always willing to play with Mom's sparkly beads and make her laugh.

Thank you to Vintaj Natural Brass for filigree used in several projects in this book.

To Linda, Cleo, Judy, and Kim—thank you for being so supportive of all my creative endeavors, from the Sheep in the Top Hat to today.

To Kiona and Leeann and all the elves of Bedizen Ornaments, thanks.

To all the talented women at Ornamentea and Panopolie—I appreciate your support, encouragement, and excitement. The emergency beading, project testing, aesthetic consultations, and calming talks made this book happen.

To the folks at Lark, who said yes to an idea and helped me figure it all out— thanks Valerie, Nathalie, and Jean. For their expert editorial assistance, thanks also to Dawn Dillingham and Kathleen McCafferty, as well as to editorial intern Halley Lawrence. I appreciate Stacey Budge's beautiful art direction, and can't say enough good things about the production assistants who kept the book smoothly on track: Jeff Hamilton, Avery Johnson, Lance Wille, and Shannon Yokeley.

Thank you to Shannon Yokeley, Jeanine Mornu, and Chevron Trading Post & Bead Co. for loaning the filigree items pictured on page 9 of the Filigree Primer.

And finally, I'm grateful for the many folks I've had the joy of working with in bead stores. You allow me to share my love of detail and sparkle, and get just as excited as I do when a bead goes right where it's supposed to.

About the Author

Cynthia Deis has been making tiny things since childhood, when she took apart garage sale jewelry to create new trinkets for her dolls. As a teenager, she changed her hair color frequently, sewed beads to her shoes, and designed outfits for her patient younger sister. She worked as a teacher and as a window-dresser before selling her jewelry professionally under the trade name Bedizen Ornaments. Her designs eventually found homes around the world through catalogs and department stores, and they have been featured in fashion magazines and worn by glamorous women.

Cynthia creates her jewelry at home while distracting her two young daughters with pet chickens, glitter, and sing-alongs. She also gardens, teaches classes, and works at her bead stores. One of her favorite things is to help beginning beaders find their creative voices.

Notes About Suppliers

Usually, you can find the supplies you need for making the projects in Lark books at your local craft supply store, discount mart, home improvement center, or retail shop relevant to the topic of the book. Occasionally, however, you may need to buy materials or tools from specialty suppliers. In order to provide you with the most up-to-date information, we have created a listing of suppliers on our website, which we update on a regular basis. Visit us at www.larkbooks.com, click on "Craft Supply Sources," and then click on the relevant topic. You will find numerous companies listed, with the web address and/or mailing address and phone number.